Beyond the Curtain into the Holy of Holies

Listening to the voice of God

LUCINDA PETERS BLACK

Copyright © 2022 LUCINDA PETERS BLACK

All rights reserved.

ISBN: 9798357988836

DEDICATION

To our Father in Heaven, Lord Jesus Christ our Savior, Yahweh, King of kings and LORD of lords, I am grateful You allowed me to journey in this magnificent plan not orchestrated by me, but Your Spirit. I give You all praise, honor, and glory!

Much appreciation to my husband, family, and friends who prayed and encouraged me through this devotional.

May blessings fall on each of you for your vital role in God's plan.

                    Shalom,
                    Lucinda

This book is intended to assist anyone who desires a deeper connection with our Father, LORD of Lords, Almighty God, and Jesus our Savior. Throughout Scripture there is a continual drawing of God's people to Himself. Why? Because God desires communion, relationship, and connection with mankind. If we evaluate our lives and relationships, a natural tendency is a desire to be loved by those in our lives. The heart of God is for us to connect with Him and to experience all He has for us. James 4:8 states (NIV), *"Come close to God and He will come close to you."* This is one of many accounts where Scripture re-enforces when we initiate our relationship with God, we will experience more of Him.

Beyond the Curtain into the Holy of Holies symbolizes our God connection from the day of Moses to our present day. To understand *this devotional,* we must revisit the story of the Ten Commandments and building of the Tabernacle.

Moses met God on Mt. Sinai where he was given the Ten Commandments written in stone (Exodus 19). Here are the Ten Commandments (in abbreviation) from Exodus 20 (NIV):

1. You shall have no other gods before Me.
2. You shall not make for yourself an idol in the form of anything in heaven above or on the earth beneath or in the waters below.
3. You shall not misuse the name of the LORD your God, for the LORD will not hold anyone guiltless who misuses his name.
4. Remember the Sabbath day by keeping it holy.
5. Honor your father and your mother, so that you may live long in the land the LORD your God is giving you.
6. You shall not murder.
7. You shall not commit adultery.
8. You shall not steal.
9. You shall not give false testimony against your neighbor.
10. You shall not covet your neighbor's house (spouse, servants, animals, anything belonging to your neighbor).

God instructed Moses to *"have them (Israelites) construct a sanctuary for Me, so that I may dwell among them"* Exodus 25:8 (NASB). This is early proof of God's desire to be among His people. Later, when Jesus came to earth we see, yet again, God's desire to be among His people. When Jesus ascended to Heaven, He informed mankind, *"But now I am going to Him who sent Me…. But I tell you the truth: it is to your advantage that I am leaving; for if I do not leave, the Helper will not come to you; but if I go, I will send Him to you"* John 16:5-7 NASB. The Helper is the Holy Spirit which is omnipresent, revealing once again God's desire to be among His people.

God instructed Moses to place the Ten Commandments in the Tabernacle, which includes specific instructions in Exodus 25-40 and includes the Holy Place and Most Holy Place, two separate areas in the Tabernacle and often referred to as the Holy of Holies. A curtain separated the two areas. The Most Holy Place is where the Ark of the Covenant was housed (Exodus 26:31-14). The Ark of the Covenant housed the Ten Commandments, a jar of manna, and Aaron's staff, otherwise known as The Testimony. There are specific details regarding the Tabernacle in Exodus chapters 25-40.

The Most Holy Place was a sacred space because God withdrew from Mt. Sinai and resided at the Tabernacle. This was purposeful so that God was portable with His people and instructed His people.

There were offerings and rituals enacted for God's people to enter the Tabernacle. The priests were responsible for the Tabernacle and God instructed Moses concerning these responsibilities. Jesus offered humanity greater insight into the Ten Commandments as well as a change in the rituals required during Moses' era.

Since Jesus' resurrection, God's Spirit came to earth to reside among His people. The Helper, or Holy Spirit, is omnipresent and available to all people all the time. Through my experience, when we engage the Holy Spirit and our sacred holy place, we will have unlimited engagements and/or experiences with our Heavenly Father. This may be attributed to James 4:8. However, this in no way means God waits for us to pursue Him. He actively pursues us!

This book intends to help you recognize our twenty-first century experience can be like the Holy of Holies if we are willing to go "Beyond the Curtain."

This book is structured as a conversation between God and the writer over topics that surprise even her at times. God's words are in *"italics and parentheses"* while the writer's words are in block writing. Often God addresses the reader by stating, "chosen one." Chosen one is significant because God wants you to know you are important to Him and chosen by Him. Consider the importance of your name by the King of kings and Lord of lords. You are chosen!

God asked me to write this book in the first quarter of 2021 for you. It is intended to draw us closer to God and into the Holy of Holies. Learn to sit with God and embrace your space while being attentive to your five senses as well as how you interact with your world. He will speak to you in ways never imagined. Embrace all aspects of life, not just what you think is appropriate or the way you think God speaks. Embrace and enjoy the connection without intention. Learn to sit with Him and be chosen!

                                          Shalom,

                                          Lucinda

DAY 1: I awake from my slumber to hear, *"come, come sit with Me again."* I know who this is – this is that same gentle, loving whisper I experienced before. Oh, what an experience! How I wish I could experience that once more. Yes! Yes! I will come with You!

I tip toe to the living room, sitting on my most comfy chair, and shut my eyes hoping to see what I saw last time. Not only do I return to that same joy-filled, peace-loving event, but this time I am handed my favorite dessert, chocolate cream pie with meringue on top. Yum. As I am searching for a spoon, that still small voice says, *"but wait, wait for Me. Enjoy this with Me. Come and follow Me. Come behind the curtain and I'll retrieve the utensils."* But wait, I thought I was already behind the curtain. *"No, My Child, there is more, and I am ready to show you what waits for you. You are ready."*

I think what more could there be and what am I ready for? This seems puzzling to me yet intriguing and exciting. *"Yes! It is exciting and the road before you will unfold one puzzle piece at a time, and I will help you."* But wait I exclaim, You heard what I thought? *"Dear chosen one, I made you and I know you better than you know yourself. Let's enjoy that pie!"*

The scarlet curtain opens and, somehow, I feel as if I entered my favorite ride at Disney World, and I am on the ride for the third time – how exciting! He invites me to sit in a fancy chair. It seems to fit me perfectly and the warmth that envelops me is beyond words. He brings forth the golden utensils and alabaster plates for our chocolate cream pie. How scrumptious the pie is as it sits on that hand carved plate.

"But not as wonderfully made as you, He stated." My head turns as if to lose my mind, He heard that!?! *"Yes, He stated, you are more wonderful than this plate. I chose you."*

Okay, okay, I'm thinking, hold myself together and enjoy this pie! I take the golden utensil He presents to me, and the chocolate cream pie on the alabaster plate, sitting on the fancy chair that envelopes me, I take a bite of the wonderful dessert. As the silky texture slides over my tongue and down my throat, I wonder how I deserve to experience such joy.

He said, *"you don't."* I said, I don't what? His loving tone states, *"you don't deserve any of this, but I give it freely because you chose to come with Me."*

I could get used to this.

DAY 2: Today I awake and feel drawn to the couch. I grab my coffee and head to the remembrance of yesterday. There is no way today could be better than yesterday. Oh yesterday. It was a delightful remembrance.

"It can be like that every day," the voice whispered.

What!?! I cannot understand how He knows what I'm thinking.

"Yes, My Child, I made you. I know you. Come with Me behind the curtain and we will sit together."

Suddenly, I feel chills run throughout my body and it feels as if His hand touches mine as I move toward the curtain. I'm not awake yet, but somehow it doesn't matter. Most definitely! It does not matter! As I enter the Most Holy Place I grab for the chair because I'm thinking I might faint. The peace this place exudes is beyond human words and the light shines brightly but does not hurt my eyes. The flood of light seems to consume my soul. I still myself into silence and all around me disappears, even my coffee. As I sit on my couch, yet in this Most Holy Place, I can see why going beyond the curtain is important. My worries seem non-existent. Maybe they are not in my thoughts because I set them down when I walked in. How did I set them down? How did I know to do that? I don't remember anyone asking me for them. All I remember is chills, a touch, and suddenly a light, and I became weak. Am I dead or alive or am I sleeping and out of it? I cannot make sense of this bizarre experience. This couch-curtain experience is unsettling yet settling. Where did He go? I thought He was with me.

"I am here, My child. I will never leave you nor forsake you. You are My chosen one. My presence is always with you because you chose to follow Me." How do You do that, be everywhere and hear everything? *"I am God. I am fully Divine. I am fully present for you but also for your friends. I exceed human comprehension. Humanity is understood by Me because I made you. Not only did I make you, but I sent My son to earth to help you more."* I don't understand, I said. *"It is okay, you are human. You will gain more understanding later."*

If this curtain experience weren't so wonderful, I would wonder about myself. I wonder why this experience is so disturbing but wonderful at the same?

"It is because you are intrigued, yet unsettled with the unknown," He replies.

I should have known He was here and will answer me. Instead of wondering I suppose I could just ask Him.

"Yes, He gently spoke. It is whatever you feel most comfortable with. I will meet you there."

Where will You meet me? I am confused.

"I will answer you in your thoughts or I will answer your questions, He calmly offered."

Okay. So, let me get this straight. I can just talk to You like I would my friend or You can also hear my thoughts.

"Yes." Do You always hear my thoughts?

"Yes." Well, that is scary. "Oh, sweet one. What a joy you are to Me. Remember, I made you. This is only scary to you because you're just learning of Me, and you do not understand My ways as I do yours."

Okay, but how will I get comfortable with you knowing my thoughts? With his gentle voice I hear, "the more you sit with Me, the more you will understand about Me. I will help you understand. Do not fret."

DAY 3: I lay in my bed wondering, what is this curtain? I do not have a curtain at my couch. Why does He say come behind the curtain?

"*Good morning, My chosen one. The curtain is a physical presence but since My son came to earth, the curtain is omnipresent and is metaphorical.*"

Metaphorical!?! Metaphorical!!! Really!?! Are You saying I did not go behind a real curtain?!? Did I eat pie?

"*Breathe, My chosen one. I will teach you. The curtain represents an entrance into the spiritual realm where you engage with Me. It is an action step on your part. It is not physical, and you do not need to walk behind a physical curtain to experience Me. However, if you want to create a curtain around your couch or anywhere that is well with My soul. You are welcome to create your physical space as you wish. Let Me explain the entrance or curtain to the spiritual realm.*"

This seems most confusing yet so peaceful. I hope I can understand this curtain thing He speaks of.

"*The entrance or curtain is metaphorical since Jesus came to earth and returned to Me. The entrance, curtain, or awareness of My presence is a choice for you since the Holy Spirit arrived. You decide when you want to engage My presence. By engaging Me, My Holy Spirit, then you step beyond the curtain into an experience comparable to what you are willing to engage. If you are a person who presents skepticism regarding life, then you most likely will present skepticism about stepping beyond the curtain. If you are a person who embraces life with wide, open opportunities then you will have a different experience. One person's experience is not better than another.*"

So, are you saying that one person gets better treatment or a different treatment from You than another?

"*Oh no, My child! Each person is equal in My eyes and created uniquely different. It brings Me great joy to interact with each person in their unique way. It is their heart to seek Me that I see.*"

I don't understand how You do not have favorites and You did call me Your chosen one.

His gentle voice holds me as He speaks, "*oh sweet one, all of those who seek Me with their heart are chosen. This does not negate how special each person is in My eyes. Being chosen means I chose you, but you also chose Me. You chose to interact with Me by stepping behind the curtain or engaging My spirit.*"

Yes. So, You are saying that every person is chosen because You made them, correct?

"Yes"

And every person is called chosen when they choose You?

"Exactly!"

I'm thinking, could it really be that simple?

"Yes, sweet one, yes," I hear softly.

DAY 4: As I gather my daily tasks and set the schedule before me, I hear Him whisper, *"take Me with you."*

Immediately I think, how do I do that? There is no curtain, no couch, but then the thought comes, *"if you think a thought and hear Me then you can be with Me all the time."*

Wow, I never imagined the ability to take Him with me wherever I went! Am I able to talk with You at any time?

His kind voice states, *"oh yes, I am everywhere, remember? If you are willing to talk to Me, no matter where you are or what you are doing then I will respond."*

All I can think is that this makes me superhuman by having the God of the universe in my thoughts. Of course, He just heard that.

"Sweet One, superhuman cannot be attained through Me, but walking with awareness of what I desire for you may bring you greater confidence in yourself"

Do I need greater confidence in myself, God?

"What you need, My child, is greater confidence in Me through you."

This is quite complicated, isn't it God?

"Not really. Humans over-complicate matters and this is no different. Greater confidence in Me means you trust Me, trust what I say to you. Through trust in Me you will gain greater confidence in yourself."

Oh Father, please help me understand how to do this. Again, his gentle whisper, *"I will."*

DAY 5: Out of nowhere I hear Him speak, *"are you willing to trust Me for the next 200 days?"*

I have many questions about this. 200 days? What does this represent and what do I need to trust You for in those 200 days? I feel as if there is much to ask before I can commit to a response.

"Oh, My child, that is why you must trust first. Trusting Me is different than trusting humans. Humans are fallible and many are not trustworthy. Please do not compare Me to them. I am God. I am different than humans."

This is not easy for me. I have trusted many people, including my dad, and I found hurt and pain from those moments of trust.

"I understand and I know those moments have hurt you greatly. I am sorry those people hurt you. That was not My plan for you."

-Pause-

"I want to show you who I am and how I created you. In order to do that, stepping into a place of trust in Me is important. I will never hurt you, Sweet One. I will not leave you nor will I forsake you. You are chosen by Me, and I have many beautiful plans for you that you cannot see."

This is extremely hard yet my experience with You has been so pleasant and peaceful.

"I understand. I will never push you to do anything you do not wish. I made humans with free will so you may exercise your rights, freedoms, and identity according to your wish. I will not force you to engage Me. However, if you do not talk with Me then our relationship will resemble a one-sided conversation. I created humans so I may have intimacy with them, and this is created by us talking to one another."

If I don't agree to trust You with the 200 days, then will You never speak to me again?

"Of course not! I understand your humanness. I will prompt you with My desire to always be your best while you are on earth. But I will not force you to interact with Me and I will leave you alone if you so desire."

This makes me sad to think I would never experience beyond the curtain again. And I do not want to do this world alone. I need You.

"This blesses Me, dear one, when you need Me. When you need Me and ask, I be with you then I will always be with you. I will unfold more than you could ever imagine when you ask."

I feel somewhat hesitant but excited and happy with curiosity to think what could be when I think of agreeing to the 200 days.

-pause-

I have decided. I am willing to trust You for 200 days.

DAY 6: As I enter the night, I feel somewhat scared of what I agreed to, but the curiosity remains. I expect to hear from God on that thought but nothing comes. I feel as if I'm being held in the warmth of a big fuzzy blanket. I drift off to sleep quickly. This morning I awake to the bright, warm sunshine through my window. It seems to bring joy to my spirit as I make my coffee and enter my secret place. I tell myself, "I am entering something new that I did not plan for nor know where I am going." Most unusually I flip open my Bible and open to Jude verse 20-21. It states, *"But you, dear friends, must build each other up in your most holy faith, pray in the power of the Holy Spirit, and await the mercy of our Lord Jesus Christ, who will bring you eternal life. In this way, you will keep yourselves safe in God's love."* Almost instantly I realize by agreeing to the 200 days I am "safe in God's love" and I have a rush of warmth fall over me. Thank You, Father, for bringing me this verse!

"Oh sweet, child. I know the desires of your heart. The safety of My love for you is important and you will continue to feel My love in various ways. Safety will be a new thought for you. Dear one, trust I have your best interests in mind."

In looking at the verse again I see the writer emphasize that I am to *"build each other up in your most holy faith"* and I wonder what this looks like. The verse states, most holy faith and reminds me of the Most Holy Place that the spirit spoke of. It sounds so similar I wonder if it is the same.

Then I hear the voice of God say, *"My child, you please Me. You please Me to seek out the written Word. The Word will guide you in understanding. The Word has weathered time. It cannot be forsaken. Carry it with you wherever you go. Carry it in your mind and in your pocket. It is My Word written for humanity until the end of time. It is for such a time as this that you are to hide the Word in your heart and soul so that you may overcome the days ahead. Trust what I have spoken. Trust Me in the days ahead."*

I feel comforted yet perplexed with the words, *"so that I may overcome the days ahead."* I am reminded that God said He has my best interests in mind. This is where I must remain! God, what do You mean by *"hiding Your Word in my heart and soul so that I may overcome the days ahead?"*

"Well, My child, the days before you may be difficult. There may be days that you do not want to exist on this earth because it will be terribly anti-God, but this is where your most holy faith will need reassurance in Me. Most holy faith is like going beyond the curtain into the Holy of Holies. It is stepping

into a deeper place of faith that is holy."

What is faith?

"Faith is like trust. Faith and trust in Me are believing in something that is unseen to the natural eye, but to spiritual sight is exposed, honored, and relished for others to see. It is like walking with blinders on yet led by another's voice. That voice is the voice of the Holy Spirit."

Can there be other voices that speak?

"Yes. There is evil in the world as well as in the spirit realm. Be attentive to My voice, the voice of the Holy Spirit. When you hear spirits other than Mine, ask Me to rid them from you so no confusion will come. I will fight for you. I am your Warrior and Advocate. Just ask and it will be given."

Oh, I am so thankful for Your omnipresence with me. Thank You for helping me to understand. I praise You!

DAY 7: I continue to ponder that verse from Jude and the words, *"build each other up in your most holy faith."* This makes me think I have a role in another's life. So, through my most holy faith I build others up?

"Yes, My chosen one, yes. When others see your most holy faith they wonder, question, and are attracted to your determined state. There may be some humans who reject you because of this but do not fret over them. They are in My hands. Focus on those coming into your sphere who wonder and question. Share life with them. Celebrate the good, grieve together, and allow My presence to overflow into their lives. It is through you that they will gain their most holy faith and it is from you that they will gain understanding from Me."

I understand. It is through faith that I demonstrate the unseen to others, and You will be present to handle the questions or uncertainties with those people, right?

"Absolutely! The Spirit is available to all people all the time. When you interact with others, they will experience something different in you and that difference is the new you that is journeying with Me. It is through you that I can speak to those people and lead them into their experience beyond the curtain into the Holy of Holies. Do not fret with performing perfectly or feelings of inadequacy for those are only deterrents from My perfect will for you. Just be yourself and trust I am with you. I will handle all matters. You are not alone. I am with you always."

A tremendous rush of peace falls upon me as I realize that my responsibilities are limited and, most importantly, I am to remain connected in this most holy faith which is like the Most Holy Place. It is about resting in His presence to experience His fullness in my life but also for others. What a relief to know that my responsibility is limited to bringing others into their experience beyond the curtain. God has me. His plan is perfect. His plan for others is perfect. Thank You, Jesus, for Your enduring and everlasting sacrifice on the cross for us.

DAY 8: As I read I Timothy 1:7, *"for God has not given us a spirit of fear and timidity, but of power, love, and self-discipline,"* the word surrender pops into my vision.

"My child, oh how I wish you could see fear in a picture. Allow Me to paint you a picture so you may see the toxicity for yourself. Fear is not from Me. This means fear is from the enemy forces of evil. Fear rides a black horse with a black cape wrapped around itself so it may disguise its ugliness from you. If you were to remove the cape you would find a sinister, evil smirk that lounges about seeking whom he may entice to agree to his fearful schemes. When you engage this sinister, evil trickster then fear emits from him and in cloud-like form gracefully falls upon you. The dark, impending cloud settles into your mind, grabs your inner being, and begins to infiltrate your senses. The cloud covers you everywhere and every thought grabs you with apprehension and uncertainty. Fear seduces you into a timid state of response."

Dear Jesus, this scares me to hear of this picture.

"I desire it awaken you, My dear one. For this is what the evil one does to distract and mislead you from My perfect will for you"

Well, it certainly awoke me! Now that I am scared, what shall I do to release the fear?

"I am with you. I will never leave you nor forsake you. All that is necessary is to call on Me. Call on Jesus! Ask Me to handle this fear and it will leave. Be reminded of the second half of this verse, 'but of power, love, and self-discipline'."

Is this where the surrender comes?

"No, surrender is your asking Me to handle the fear. Many people think they must be stronger to be a child of God, but this is not true. Surrender to God brings power, love, and self-discipline. Do you understand?"

I think so. It is somewhat confusing to consider surrender brings power.

"Surrender to Me brings My power in you in a supernatural way that cannot be understood, but it must be experienced. Love will ensue and self-discipline will follow once you experience the power of God in you. It is through this power that you will recognize that self-discipline becomes a wonderful process of obedience."

"Trust the plan before you. Remember that when the evil of fear falls upon you to call on Jesus."

DAY 9: Oh, dear God, why do I have such anxiety?

"Because you need to de-clutter your mind and your space."

God, I have so much to do that it is hard to understand how to de-clutter my mind.

"My child, to experience true peace, then you will benefit from hearing John's words. John 5:25 states, 'Truly, truly, I say to you, a time is coming and even now has arrived, when the dead will hear the voice of the Son of God, and those who hear will live.' You see, to be alive, you must hear Jesus' voice and to hear Jesus' voice then you must de-clutter your mind to hear from heaven. And, from this experience you will gain tremendous peace."

I want to feel alive! But how do I de-clutter my mind?

"De-cluttering the mind is like de-cluttering a home. One must decide what to keep and what to throw away. Determine what is important to retain. We often retain trash in our thoughts that clutter our thinking. Determine what you can throw away and rid your mind of unwanted trash. In this process, what is kept must be organized and put in a system of order. Order and ridding of one's clutter provide space for one to hear and feel alive."

Beyond the curtain:
Determine the top 3 areas of clutter you allow in your **Thoughts** and in your **Sacred Space** that causes anxiety and keeps you from hearing from the Lord.

Clutter Thoughts:
1._____
2._____
3._____

Clutter in your Sacred Space:
1._____
2._____
3._____

What is ONE step in each area you can act on today to experience freedom in your mind and spirit?

Clutter Thought: Choose one thought where you have no control that can be changed today. Choose this thought and set it down at the heavenly throne. Pray: Jesus, please take this thought from me. I need Your help.
I surrender this to you _____

Sacred Space clutter: Choose one thing you can change in your sacred space to give you more comfort and peace. You may need to add or remove something like a color, smell, or sound (five senses: sight, smell, taste, touch, sound). Make your space yours and the way you need it in order to commune with the Father.

DAY 10: When I awake, I feel an overwhelming sense of fear. Fear of losing my job, my home, my family, everything! Where did this come from?

"Oh, Beautiful one, fear is not from Me. I know fear well, but it is only as big as you allow. When you feel fear, you must not embrace the fear but release it to My care. I am bigger than the fear inside you. I am the everlasting God, King of kings and Lord of lords. I am far greater than the fear inside you. Hand it to Me."

Oh God, I am so tired. I am tired of this world, the demands, and the pressures of the day.

"I understand. These pressures and demands create fear. Fear of not being enough, fear of rejection, fear of uncertainty, fear of loss, or fear of failure. All of these feel real. But the reality is I AM greater than these fears. This is what you must begin to trust. Trust that I am greater."

How do I trust You in this way?

"In your sacred place, find a Bible verse that you identify with."

Beyond the curtain:
Pray: Dear Jesus, open my eyes to see what You want me to see. Help me choose the best verse for me. Amen.

Jeremiah 29:11 *"For I know the plans I have for you, says the Lord. They are plans for good and not for disaster, to give you a future and a hope."*

Philippians 4:6-7 *"Do not be anxious about anything, but in everything by prayer and pleading with thanksgiving let your requests be made known to God. And the peace of God, which surpasses all comprehension, will guard your hearts and minds in Christ Jesus."*

Proverbs 30:5 *"Every word of God proves true. He is a shield to all who come to Him for protection."*

John 3:30 *"He must become greater and greater, and I must become less and less."*

Galatians 2:20 *"My old self has been crucified with Christ. It is no longer I who live, but Christ lives in me. So, I live in this earthly body by trusting in the Son of God, who loved me and gave himself for me."*

Once you have chosen your verse then do these three things:

1. *Write the verse(s) on paper and post around your home*
2. *Replace the fear inside you with your chosen verse(s)*
3. *Whenever fear arises within you, take your fear and align it with your chosen verse(s)."*

What is my goal, God? To live fear-free?

"Your goal, My chosen one, is to live in communion with Me, to live intimately with Me, the One who made you, knows you, and has a plan for your life. Fear may come and go but I will never leave you. Seek Me in every moment and I will always be there. I will ALWAYS be there."

Notes:

DAY 11: *"Awaken, My chosen one! There is hope for tomorrow!"*

What is hope, God?

"Hope is defined, in old times, as trust in something. Hope is expectation that good will come. Do you see that trust in Me brings hope?"

I do. Trust is hard, is it not?

"Trust in Me is often hindered because of humanity's pain executed on one another. Much of humanity has little trust in others, even themselves. This brings difficulty in trusting Me, but it is not impossible. Remember when I taught you about going "beyond the curtain" into the Holy of Holies, and you followed?"

Yes.

"That is trust. You trusted that I had good for you, and you followed."

True.

"This is no different. Trusting that all I have for you is good brings you into a deeper relationship with Me."

I think I see now. My relationship with You is like my relationship with other people. But You are more trustworthy. And, if I have been hurt by someone in my life then that may make it more difficult to trust You. Did I miss anything?

"Dear Chosen One, you are learning quickly. Remind yourself that trust in Me brings hope for tomorrow. Hope for tomorrow is an everlasting continuum that brings hope for today and tomorrow."

Beyond the curtain:
Surround yourself with a <u>color</u> that brings hope for today....and tomorrow!

DAY 12: I feel defeated today. How can I overcome this thought, Lord? I cannot accomplish all that is before me. It seems overwhelming.

"Do you know I am asking you to accomplish this task? Do you know I am asking you to set aside other priorities to accomplish this task?" Yes. I understand this truth, but the demands seem great.

"Where do Your demands come from?" People. *"And where else?"* My insecurities? That I will not finish what I started. That the task is too big. I am old and tired.

"Let us evaluate these statements. Do you tend to start something without finishing it?"

Well, I usually finish the task, but it may take longer than I like.

"Ok. Second evaluation. Is this task too big for you to finish?"

It feels too big. But realistically, if I break it into pieces and stay steady then it can be accomplished.

"Lastly, are you old and tired?" Sometimes I feel old and tired.

"It appears to Me that you are tempted to believe lies about yourself and what I have asked you to do. These lies must be defeated with My Truth. Your task is a large one so you must determine to re-organize your schedule to accommodate the needs to accomplish the task. When I have called you to a task this may mean eliminating people time, phone time, and internet surfing. Your priority is what I have asked of you. Utilize your 'do not disturb' and quiet place to accomplish all I have asked. Lastly, apply My Truth to these lies so they do not grow roots into your thoughts."

Proverbs 4:23, *"Guard your heart above all else, for it determines the course of your life."*

Ezekiel 3:17, *"Son of man, I have appointed you ..."*

Hebrews 13:5-6, *"For God said, I will never fail you. I will never abandon you…the Lord is my helper, so I will have no fear."*

Beyond the curtain:
What is your lie? _____
Apply the Truth to your lie: _____

DAY 13: I feel hunger in my stomach.

"My Chosen One, what do you hunger for?"

I know I feel hunger. This makes me think I need food. But I hunger to hear from You.

"Do you understand our relationship? It is one where you seek Me when you hunger."

Lord, Lord, what am I to do? I want to be in communion with You. I know I seek You. I listen to You. But I wait on You to awaken me.

"Child, child, learn from the wisdom of Your Father. I am warmed by your thoughts of seeking Me. Yes! Of course, I will seek you. Your seeking brings warmth as after a summer rain."

Father, please forgive me.

"You are forgiven. Remember to seek Me. I will seek you. We will seek one another. Intentionality is the root of our relationship. If you seek to be intentional in our relationship, then there will be change that comes in every aspect of your life."

Lord, help me to understand how to live out this relationship with You. I need You.

"I am with you always. I will never leave you nor forsake you."

Beyond the curtain:

Dear God, I agree and commit to seek You (circle one) **daily, weekly, or monthly**. I need Your help to understand how to connect and hear from You. Please show me how.

Turn to Proverbs and go to the chapter that coincides with the day of the month for the date of today. Find a verse in that chapter that you identify with and write it down as a reminder of this agreement. If you write in your Bible, then underline or highlight that verse. Put the date and a small note to remind yourself of this moment.

Chosen verse: _____

Pray: God, I give You praise, honor, and glory! Thank You for speaking to me today. Amen.

DAY 14: *"My child, My child, listen to My words. Obedience to My Word, the Bible is never ending and forever rewarding. Seek always to serve with obedience and My rewards will be great."*

What must I do to remain obedient?

"Follow Me daily through every moment of your life. Seek to please Me, your Father in Heaven."

"Yesterday, you learned to commit yourself to Me. Often the moment-to-moment listening and communing with Me is valuable to many. The moment-to-moment connection to the Spirit is a comfort and a gentle embrace amid chaos."

Father, I am afraid I will not perfect the plan between us.

"Oh, Chosen One, perfection cannot be achieved by anyone. The outcome is not the focus but the heart attitude of the seeker. Do you remember King David when he was chosen to be the king? I told Samuel as he was choosing the king to 'look at the heart, for people look at outward appearance but My ways are different than worldly ways' (I Samuel 17:7)."

You are saying because my heart is pure and desires to obey you then I am chosen?

"Yes, My Chosen One. Rest in this purity of the heart for not all persons are capable of such measure. Do not let anyone corrupt the purity of your heart for many are cruel and steal from the soul of the chosen. Protect the beauty of your heart for it is sacred."

How do I protect my heart?

"Remain connected to Me, allow only that which is pure to enter your heart, and do not seek to please people but Me, your Father in heaven."

Beyond the curtain:
I choose today to not let anyone steal my pure heart. I will protect myself by:

Write your protection statement as a reminder to yourself and place it in locations (car, wallet, bathroom, pocket, desk, etc.). You are a prize to be protected!

DAY 15: *"My child, many people assume Truth is relevant to the person and their perspective. Truth is My Word the Bible. It was written centuries ago by people who served Me, served Jesus."*

That was a long time ago. It seems that our world may be different than it was during Jesus' time.

"There are natural changes such as automobiles, electricity, and modern amenities. However, the Truth in which a person follows to determine answers to life is no different."

Help me understand, Father.

"Read John 3."

> *Jesus responded and said to him, "Truly, truly, I say to you, unless someone is born again, he cannot see the kingdom of God." Nicodemus said to Him, "How can a person be born when he is old? He cannot enter his mother's womb a second time and be born, can he?" Jesus answered, "Truly, truly, I say to you, unless someone is born of water and the Spirit, he cannot enter the kingdom of God. That which has been born of the flesh is flesh, and that which has been born of the Spirit is spirit. Do not be amazed that I said to you, 'You must be born again.' The wind blows where it wishes, and you hear the sound of it, but you do not know where it is coming from and where it is going; so is everyone who has been born of the Spirit."* (NASB)

"Dear Chosen One, these spoken words from Jesus represent My heart for every person on the earth. Jesus came to earth, died, and resurrected for one purpose, to make a way for every person to enter heaven. This choice is for every person and this choice matters whether the world has internet or not, electric cars or not, candles or electricity. Every person who is born does so whether it is in a barn or a hospital. Death is no different. Every person will take one last breath to exit this world and enter heaven or hell. Life and death are for every person no matter what. However, the life lived between these two bookends is either in the Spirit or the flesh. It is your choice."

Jesus said in verse 5 that I must be born of water and the Spirit. Is this different than going "beyond the curtain?"

"Born of the water is a public display of commitment to Christ where one receives baptism by water. Born of the spirit is similar and allows an ongoing connection to Me, the Father."

You are saying if I learn to live "beyond the curtain," it is the same as connecting with the Spirit and like the wind? Is it a day-to-day experience, with the most important aspect being to engage the Spirit and not my fleshly desire?

"Yes!"

Beyond the curtain:
Pray: Dear God, Lord Jesus, Holy Spirit, help me to live like the wind with the Spirit and not my fleshly desires. I surrender to Your Lordship.

What fleshly desire is the Spirit asking you to surrender?

DAY 16: Today I ponder the thought of giving up my fleshly desire. There seem to be many. I desire to teach the children in Sunday School, sing in the choir, and serve the homeless. Are these my desires or a calling upon my life?

"Which of these things cause you to focus on yourself more than the Spirit through you?"

When I consider each of these, there is much but it seems when I sing, I am hindered by how I appear and serving the homeless feels like an obligation. But as I consider the children, they are pure of heart, vulnerable, and need a safe person to care for them. When I leave class, I feel happy and invigorated in my day.

"The invigoration represents the Spirit in you that brightens your day and brings joy."

Does this mean my flesh engages serving in the choir or serving the homeless people?

"It does for now and this may change. For the moment, your time may best be served by stepping away from those obligations."

I will follow You, God. However, I agreed to sing in the choir for a specific period and I do not want to let my friends down.

"My Chosen One, hard decisions come to those who serve Me, and choices must be made. Look at Matthew 8:19-22,

> *"Then a scribe came and said to Him, 'Teacher, I will follow You wherever You go.' And Jesus said to him, 'The foxes have holes and the birds of the sky have nests, but the Son of Man has nowhere to lay His head.' And another of the disciples said to Him, 'Lord, allow me first to go and bury my father.' But Jesus said to him, 'Follow Me, and let the dead bury their own dead.'" (NASB)*

Wow! I want to follow You, God. Can I not go to funerals if I follow You?

"My Sweet One, this merely emphasizes the importance to follow the Spirit wherever you are led. Remember it is as the wind blows that the Spirit moves."

Beyond the curtain:
What might you be doing in your life that satisfies your flesh? What changes do you need to make in your life to follow the Spirit?

Jesus, help me to be strong in the Spirit and make these changes so I can go where you call me.

DAY 17: There are days when God says nothing. As I sit in my sacred place, I feel His presence. I hear the birds chirping. I feel peace. I see warmth as it falls upon the day. God are You with me?

"My Chosen One, I am always with you. I will never leave you nor forsake you."

Why do You not speak on some days?

"It is My desire to connect My people with their surroundings and see that I am there too. What do you connect with today?"

The birds chirping. They sound happy.

"I made many birds of the air. They seek to please Me by building their nests. They ready themselves for what is yet to come. How do you seek to please Me?"

You say the birds please You with their nest building, then how am I to please You?

"You please Me by doing whatever you do best. If you serve, serve well. If you teach, teach well. So it is that whatever you do best then do it as unto Me, your Father in Heaven. (Romans 12)"

My soul sits quietly in my sacred place pondering the movement around me with consideration that God is present.

Beyond the curtain:
Bring your awareness to your environment. What do you notice that represents God?
_____
_____
_____
_____

What do you do well and can please God with your service?
_____
_____
_____
_____

DAY 18: God, why did Balaam's donkey talk? (Numbers 22, 2 Peter 2:16)

"Sometimes I must use bizarre acts to get people's attention. This was one of those moments."

What did Balaam do for You to use such an act?

"Balaam was called to give My Word to people. He is My representative and called to honor what I say. I instructed Balaam 'not to go' and he did not listen. Through his disobedience I used his donkey to remind him of My words, but he still did not listen. When he beat his donkey, My instrument of instruction, the next measure of awareness was to have the donkey speak."

This seems no different in our day as compared to Balaam. In what ways do You move that people miss?

"I send people for assistance and help is refused. I give word to My prophets, and they do not listen. I close doors and people force them open. I bring people to moments that they deny. I create opportunities to share Jesus' love and people ignore this foundation of Truth."

Why do people find it difficult to see You move among them?

"Humanity embraces control, self-sufficiency, misunderstanding, insecurity, and fear. These are distractions to My perfect plan for them."

How do we change this part of us?

"One must surrender to Me daily, even minute-by-minute. This takes persistent attention to the Spirit as it moves among you. Once surrendered, then one can walk in obedience to what is before them just as I asked Balaam 'not to go'."

Beyond the curtain:
What is God asking you to surrender? _____

Pause and ask the Spirit what obedient act is for you? _____

Affirmative Action: I will surrender _____
and be obedient to do _____
as God is asking. Lord, help me to follow through on these actions. Amen.

DAY 19: As I sit this morning, I feel as if there is more for me to do. God, how do I know what You want me to do in this world?"

"Chosen One, what is it that when you do it you experience satisfaction and accomplishment?"

But God, should it be more than that?

"Every person is unique. I created each person differently so that the world operates efficiently."

You are suggesting that there are people who find satisfaction in cleaning bathrooms or working as trash operators?

"A person is given roles and responsibilities for them to fulfill the needs of the world, but through this process that person gains confidence in oneself. Serving with a grateful heart brings joy to the soul and deeper connection with Me."

What should I focus on to follow Your plan for my future?

"Focus on connecting with Me every day, every moment so that you hear My voice. Serve with gratefulness (def: appreciative of benefits received) being mindful of all the benefits given to you such as money for food/home/car, connection with people, helping people, providing a need in the community, etc. What you do with this gift will impact your progression for bigger goals in the Kingdom of God."

God, help me to be attentive to the benefits before me so I may honor You with my heart and work.

Beyond the curtain:
What do you take for granted in your daily life that you would like to be grateful for?
_____
_____

Pick your favorite verse from this list or find one for yourself to reflect a grateful heart. Write it down, memorize it, and connect your heart to fulfil this verse and your connection with God.

Psalm 7:17	Psalm 9:1	Psalm 35:18	Psalm 69:30
Psalm 95:1-3	Psalm 100:4-5	Psalm 106:1	

Affirmative statement: I choose today to celebrate life. I celebrate the abilities God gave me.

DAY 20: *"Chosen One, Chosen One, rest in Me."*

Oh Father, fall upon me with Your presence, Your Holy Spirit, that I may experience greatness in the spirit.

"Sweet One, do not fear. I will never leave you nor forsake you. I am with you always."

Oh, how I love this calming presence of Yours upon me.

"It is what's available to you when you sit with Me."

Father, why do I not experience this more?

"Because you allow the world to distract you from My plans. Start your day with Me and I will direct your steps. You will experience the peace that passes all understanding and gain great wisdom for every decision."

Help me to make time for this so I may begin every day with peace and joy that supersedes this earth.

"Seek Me, My Child, and you will gain all you need."

Beyond the curtain:

Luke 11:9 "So I say to you, ask, and it will be given to you; seek, and you will find; knock, and it will be opened to you.

What can you do to rearrange your day to spend time with God?

How much time do you spend with God? _____ (minutes/hours)

If you desire to increase your time with God, what is the total amount? _____ (minutes/hours)

How can you accomplish your goal?   Get up earlier [ ]   Go to bed later [ ]   Use my lunch break [ ]   Ask someone to watch the children [ ]   Something else? _____

Prayer: Lord Jesus, I ask for Your help to see how I can rearrange my day to spend more time with You. Please show me how. Amen.

DAY 21: God, how hard is it to walk in Your Truth, the Bible?

"Oh, sweet one, if you focus on stepping "beyond the curtain" into your sacred place then My spirit will guide you and the journey will not be complicated nor hard."

That seems easy.

"It can be easy. However, at times, life will throw us challenges. This may come with relationships or colleagues. When we interact with other people there will be circumstances arise that can create frustration and irritation. If you agree to this interruption, then it will hinder your relationship with Me."

I feel the importance to defend myself if I am attacked by someone.

"Remember, you are not a citizen of this world (Philippians 3:20) and when you are attacked by someone it is better to find your space with Me. Talk with Me about this before responding. I will guide you. I will defend you. There are times when you will need to speak to others, but it is important to use the words I give you."

Beyond the curtain:

Who do you allow to bring frustration into your life? _____

Read these verses: Galatians 2:11-13, James 1:19-25, James 3:13-18, Proverbs 5:1-9

Why does this person have power over you?
    Do you have expectations you have placed on this person?
        If so, what are those expectations?

    Has this person placed expectations on you?
        If so, what?

    Is there a lack of communication?
        If so, what needs to be discussed?

Do I need to forgive myself, a person, or God? (it is either yes or no) _____
    If so, repeat this statement as many times as needed:
    Dear God, I forgive _____ for _____.

What can I do differently to prevent disruption in my relationship with God?

DAY 22: *"Dear one, consider being honest with yourself about who you are and what I am calling you to do in this world."*

This scares me to consider what you might ask me to do.

"Remember, My Chosen One, My plan for you is not to harm you nor cause you pain."

But who am I?

"You are chosen by Me to do what no one else can do except you."

Beyond the curtain:

Pray: Dear God, help me to see myself as You see me. Remove any fear, lack, shame, or pride. Amen.

Evaluate your strengths and write them down:
    Spiritual strengths:

    Identity strengths:

    Physical strengths:

When you consider your whole self, where are you capable of doing more than you are currently?

Where do you feel confidence, joy, or excitement when you look back at your strengths?

Where does your joy/confidence/excitement intersect with your capability?

Are there new insights, hopes, or dreams that God suggested?

What can you do to be honest with yourself and step into God's plan for your life?

DAY 23: Oh Jesus, I feel great joy in my heart today.

"What will you do with the joy you have in your heart? Will you praise? Will you celebrate? Will you share your joy with others?"

I never thought of what I would do with my joy.

"I created joy because it is an infectious response that many people need."

I give You praise, Father! You amaze me how You orchestrate the moves in my life. I celebrate You, Father!!!

"The joy in your heart is not to be stored for yourself but to spread like jam on bread. The sweetness will spread, and you will gain even more joy as you share."

But how do I do this?

"It is like walking "beyond the curtain." You are to allow Me to lead you then allow My Spirit to manifest the moment. You cannot make anything happen, but you can surrender to Me and follow wherever I go."

Lord, help me to relinquish control so I may share the joy You put in my heart.

Beyond the curtain:

Pray: Dear God, give me insight as I read Your Word.

Psalm 16:11
You will make known to me the way of life; In Your presence is fullness of joy; In Your right hand there are pleasures forever.

Proverbs 15:23
A person has joy in an apt answer, and how delightful is a timely word!

Isaiah 61:10
I will rejoice greatly in the Lord, my soul will be joyful in my God; For He has clothed me with garments of salvation, He has wrapped me with a robe of righteousness, As a groom puts on a turban, And as a bride adorns herself with her jewels.

Which verse speaks to you?

What do you **commit** to do with joy in your heart?

If you lack joy in your heart, pray this prayer:
Dear Jesus, Father God, and Holy Spirit, I need Your help. I need joy. I surrender to You completely. I ask You to show me what I need to change in my life to experience joy. In return, I will share that joy with others. Thank You for hearing my prayer. Amen.

DAY 24: God, how did You make the ocean?

"with one hand"

You amaze me. That is hard to fathom. <long pause>   I give You all praise, honor, and glory!

"What do I desire most from My people?"

Obedience?

"No."

Long thinking pause ... communion?

"Yes! I want My people to talk with Me and to spend time with Me no matter how silly a question may be. To ask questions of Me and to sit with Me brings great joy. Invite Me into every moment and great things will happen."

Your sweetness that falls upon me is lovely. I never want to leave time with You.

"You don't have to."

I love You, God.

Beyond the curtain:

What can you do to be intentional about connecting with God?

Do you have a place that helps you connect with God? The beach? The mountains? A waterfall? Driving?

When can you set aside a longer time to spend with God – like 1 day, 3 days, week, etc.?

Do you need an accountability partner to hold you to this? If so, who is it?

Pray this prayer:
Dear God, I want to be with You. I want to talk and listen with You. I ask You to provide the time and money needed so I can be with You. Thank You for hearing my prayer. Amen.

DAY 25: God, why do some people not hear from You?

"Many of My children THINK they do not hear Me, but their thoughts may be Me. They must learn to distinguish between their mind and the mind of God."

How?

"Learn to sit and quiet themselves. If every thought and emotion is taken captive through the blood of Christ, what else remains but Me and them. Right?"

Yes.

"Learn to distinguish what is manifested from oneself versus thoughts from Me."

Beyond the curtain:
Pray: Father, Lord Jesus, I ask that You take captive every thought and emotion that they may be obedient to Your name (2 Cor 10:5). I surrender to You and ask for You to help me learn to sit with You. Amen.

What can you do to "sit and quiet yourself" for the Lord to speak?

What do you see as a hindrance to this happening?

Is this hindrance something you feel pressured to do?

Consider your priorities and evaluate what you can change so you can sit and hear God's voice:
1. _____
2. _____
3. _____
4. _____

* Star anything above that needs re-ordering.

Matthew 6: 33-34 "But seek first His kingdom and His righteousness, and all these things will be provided to you. So do not worry about tomorrow; for tomorrow will worry about itself. Each day has enough trouble of its own."

DAY 26: *"Do you seek security in your life?"*

Yes, Father. Security of the unknown things, as well as those You have promised. *"The way to security of the heart is to trust in Me. Trust what you know I say to you."*

How do I lay the insecurity down?

"You must know I am greater than the insecurity you feel. Insecurity belongs to this world and human constraints. I am far greater."

Father, please give me a visual.

"You sit in the middle of a boat in the sea. The waves begin to rock the boat. Your focus is on the boat but if you look beyond the boat outward to sea you find there is great calm amidst the power. You must focus beyond yourself, beyond the immediate insecurity into the greater picture. Focus on the calm that has great power and that is Me."

Lord, please help me to step into the calm and security of Your presence during uncertainty.

Beyond the curtain:

Pray: Lord, thank You for being patient with me and accepting me the way I am. Help me to surrender my insecurities and all my unknowns so I may step into trusting You.
Find a Bible verse that brings you comfort and trust in God. (Psalm 91, Matthew 11:28, Philippians 4:6-7)
What is your verse?

What circumstances bring insecurity in your boat?

Look beyond your boat of insecurities into the calm of God's power. What do you see?

If you see nothing different, then stop and take several deep breaths. See yourself in the boat. Begin to look beyond the immediate into the calm. Stay there for as long as you like. Allow our Father in heaven to speak calm and power into your soul.

Repeat when necessary.

DAY 27: *"The wind is unseen, but it provides something important to you."*

I do not understand.

"The wind and the Holy Spirit are similar. They both are unseen yet offer support during times of trouble. Does the wind blow the pollen, so it does not lay to cause harm to the body? So does the Spirit move to bring encouragement, strength, and calm among My people."

How do we know when the Spirit is present, Father?

"At times, you may not know for the gentleness of the Spirit seeks to reside. At other moments, you may feel, think, or experience in some way different than normal. This difference may feel peaceful, but it may bring urgency."

Why would the Spirit bring urgency? Is peace not my goal?

"There are times when peace is necessary but there are times when you must recognize the importance of doing something amidst your circumstance. This is when the Spirit may place urgency in your spirit."

How will I know?

"Remember, My Chosen one, that you followed Me beyond the curtain with trust. It is trust that will guide you in the days ahead. You are to always remember where you came from not to forget the simplicity of our relationship."

Thank You, Father. Thank You so much.

Beyond the curtain:
Pray: Dear God, bring to my mind moments when the Spirit was with me.
Ponder the past and consider when the Spirit was with you, yet you may not have recognized the moment.

Do you recall any moments?

Pray: Lord, please forgive me for not recognizing when the Spirit is with me. Help me to learn to flow with the Spirit in my life. Help me to be mindful of Your presence with me. Thank You greatly. Amen.

DAY 28: God, why is humility so hard?

"Humbleness is not the way of the world. The world seeks to destroy God's people. The world builds power, control, and ego. These do not fit in My kingdom. You live in the world, but you must learn to separate yourself from the world."

It seems I am so busy trying to live and keep my head above water that it is difficult to separate myself from the world around me.

"Perhaps the busyness seeks to keep You from Me."

How do I separate myself from the world?

"First, recognize that you live in a flawed world. There are many things seeking your attention. Second, make a determined choice to change what seeks to busy you. Third, put into place a plan to focus on our relationship."

How does this apply to humility?

"Your surrender to My plan brings humility. Your humility symbolizes you need My help. When you surrender to Me, I will move mountains before you."

Beyond the curtain:
What seeks to keep you busy that needs to be changed?

* _____
* _____
* _____

What can YOU change to reduce the busyness in your world?

What mountain before you do you present to GOD for His attention to reduce the busyness?

Pray: God, I surrender to You completely. I lay before You the busyness in my life. I need Your help. Give me wisdom and insight to see what I can do and for those things I have no power over, I ask that You move the mountains before me. I praise You in advance for answering my prayer. In Jesus name, Amen.

DAY 29: God, what should my prayer be?

"I awake today to praise You, Father. I awake today to serve You and Your Kingdom. I surrender to You wholly and completely. You are my God. I am Yours."

Is this what every person should pray?

"Each person needs to recognize who they are, who I am, and where I am asking them to live their life … a dedication to Me."

So, as if we are in service to You?

"The world needs each of you walking in fulfillment of who you are. Your role is vital. The people of the earth need love. Love your neighbor as yourself." (Mark 12:28-34)

It seems our world has shut off relationships and communication.

"Do not let fear hold you captive from becoming who I created you to be."

Beyond the curtain:

Who were you created to be?

If you do not know then it may be time to begin sifting through your strengths and weaknesses. All people have strengths, and all people have weaknesses. Determine what they are and choose to walk in your strengths. Your strengths ARE who God created you to be. There is no need to be someone you are not.

Finish this sentence: I decide today to be who I am. I know I am strong in _____, _____, and _____.
Pray: Lord, help me to walk in who You created me to be. Help me to recognize my strengths that are different than other people. Give me Godly confidence, wisdom, and discernment. Thank You, Jesus. Amen.

To understand more about yourself consider taking a personality quiz. Here are a few sites that offer personality quizzes. I suggest the Myers-Briggs test from the first two options. The enneagram has become popular and gives a different perspective than the Myers-Briggs.
www.personalityhacker.com			https://enneagramtest.net

DAY 30: *"Chosen one, awaken and listen. It is My desire to teach you today so you may be stronger in the faith."*

I stumble from bed to my sacred place with the Father. I am half awake, but I hear him, and I want more.

"Obedient one, the days before you are challenging but I am with you."

This is scary.

"Do not fear. Fear is not from Me. I have much to share today. You have overcome great obstacles. It is time to understand what you have experienced on this earth can fade when you focus in your spirit. Your spirit is your strength. Your spirit can connect with My spirit, the Holy Spirit."

How do I do that?

"You already are. Learn to distinguish My voice from the others that bombard your mind. Be reminded to pray as Ephesians 6 states by placing your armor on. This will guard your mind and spirit."

Lord, I feel my mind is busy and racing. How do I slow it down to connect with the Holy Spirit?

"This is the importance of having a sacred place. This will allow you to set your racing thoughts down so your spirit may connect with the Holy Spirit. Relax, breathe, and settle into the moment. Just sit and ask Me to speak to you remembering to relax. There are no objectives or goals, only moments of connection with no pressure or expectation. Learn to rest in that spirit connection."

(long pause with connection to the Holy Spirit). Write down what you hear from the Father.

Listening is hard.

"Surrender is hard. Once surrender is understood then listening will happen. Be patient with yourself. I am with you. I will never leave you nor forsake you. I am yours and you are Mine."

Beyond the curtain:
What is the most important aspect to remember from today's experience?

What is the most frustrating aspect from today's experience?

Pray: Lord, I surrender to You. I need Your help to connect with the Holy Spirit. Please help me. Help me to set down my racing thoughts and to hear Your voice. I need You. Thank You, Father, Lord Jesus, and Holy Spirit. Amen.

DAY 31: Lord, I want to be a pure, unhindered vessel for Your Kingdom.

"Do you realize what this means?"

Probably not.

"It means whatever is not pure in your vessel must be removed. Many people are unable to allow this process to happen. Are you willing?"

(pause with evaluation and contemplation)

Lord, I admit this is not easy to consider. I surrender to You completely, but I need Your strength and help in this area.

"You cannot surrender completely without the surrender of the impurity."

Oh, snap.

"You are My honest servant. I honor your desire, but truth must be extended in the difficult places."

I see the impurity and I see how it obstructs my progress and growth with You. Lord, please help me in this area of weakness.

"My grace is all you need. My power works best in weakness. (II Cor. 12:9)"

Beyond the curtain:
Pray: Lord, I need Your help. I accept Your help. I am weak so I receive Your power and grace. I surrender to You completely.

What do you need to surrender?

How hard is it to surrender – on a scale of 1-10 (10 is the highest)? _____

Read II Corinthians 12:1-10. Paul authored II Corinthians. What takeaway from Paul's writing helps you in your surrender?

What part of these verses do you want to remember to help you overcome the impurity in your life?

Where can you post this verse as a reminder to help you through this challenge?

Do you need to talk with someone for support in this journey? If so, whom?

Encourage yourself with this statement:
God is my strength. He will never leave me nor forsake me. He will help me overcome _____. I give Him praise!

DAY 32: Father, I need You.

"I am with you always. I will never leave you nor forsake you. Come to Me, ask, and I will give you what you need."

Father, I sit and sip coffee on my comfy couch wrapped in my fleece blanket. With Your presence, this is a lovely place to be.

"Yes, yes! Surrounding yourself with My presence, the Holy Spirit, with invitation of My presence, and bringing your environment into this moment is of most importance."

Beyond the curtain:

Pause to take in the moment – aware of what you feel, taste, touch, smell, hear, and see.

Go here for a video to help you calm and connect with the Holy Spirit: https://drive.google.com/file/d/1GDbgt33e3Y0i1k2OEcATWj5GlJdeBu_c/view?usp=sharing

What do you feel the Spirit is speaking to you?

What do you think is the most important aspect of this experience?

What did you experience that you would like to continue to include in your routine with Jesus?

Was it difficult to relax? Difficult to set aside racing thoughts? If so, consider including a daily routine of meditation to include the Holy Spirit. Studies show that meditation will rebuild the grey matter in the brain. Imagine how much better it is with Jesus' inclusion!

If you feel you need more meditation, then consider when you can include it in your daily routine. Remember, this is crucial to your well-being. Meditations can be 30 seconds, 2 minutes, 5 minutes, and longer! There really is no excuse. Placing a priority on yourself is important!

Note to self:

DAY 33: God, why are numbers important to you?

"Numbers represent finality. They are absolute and need no explanation."

Do you use them to speak to your people?

"I use them in situations when a person needs them. This is intended to affirm the connection between Myself and a person. What is the number of the Godhead?"

Three – the Father, Son, and Holy Spirit.

"Excellent. How many times has three been important to you?"

In recent years, I learned that You use three similar events to affirm direction for me. Is this true?

"Yes. I allowed three people to speak into your life regarding a necessary training. They were random events orchestrated by Me. You were not looking for answers, but your heart was open to My will. Thus, I brought three people (two were strangers) into your life so that it brought attention to the topic. The third person, being trustworthy and known by you, brought the affirmation needed for you to pursue the goal."

It seems some people look at every number in front of them to use it as guidance from You. That seems somewhat scary to me.

"Some people are desperate for answers from Me. Sometimes I do offer numbers but what is most important is the heart that is seeking. The heart of My followers is seen by Me. The relationship My follower cultivates with Me will develop a well-nurtured soil for harvesting fruit from our relationship. This fruit may result in numbers or any other form of communication with My people. I know the heart of My people and I will meet them there if they will seek Me."

The 'if-then' stands out to me. Is an 'if-then' scenario important for us to recognize?

"The 'if-then' you speak of correlates to 'if a person' responds 'then I' will ..."

Does that mean You do not respond if a person does not initiate?

"That is not accurate. Sometimes, I initiate and other times I want to see people initiate. Consider the verse in II Chronicles 7:14-16, 'Then if My people who are called by My name will humble themselves and pray and seek My face and turn from their wicked ways, I will hear from heaven and will forgive

their sins and restore their land. My eyes will be open and My ears attentive to every prayer made in this place. For I have chosen this Temple and set it apart to be holy – a place where My name will be honored forever. I will always watch over it, for it is dear to My heart.' This verse describes the heart I seek from My people for they are a temple of the Spirit."

Beyond the curtain:
What part of your heart needs attention?

Pray: Lord, I confess and repent that I need help with _____. I ask for Your forgiveness and healing. Help me to change and see what You want and what is best for me. Thank You, Jesus. Amen.

DAY 34: *"What do you hunger for?"*

Coffee. And, to sit in my special place with You.

"What if I ask you to give up your coffee…"

That would be hard for me.

"Yes, yes it would."

Why would I be asked to give it up?

"My chosen one, when you are chosen and when you are ordained for a purpose under heaven, your temple is residence for the Spirit to reside (1 Cor 6:19). Your body is established as part of three unique aspects of humanity – the body, soul, and spirit. The body is often neglected by the Christ follower."

Why is this true?

"As believers in Christ, you are merely human who work diligently to follow Me. Thus, your spirit is in communion with Me and most often functions well. Your soul is your identity. Many people struggle with their identity and the implications from earthly abuse to their soul. Third, the body. The body is often that place where My people cannot see or feel the implications from their choices. Thus, it goes unnoticed to eventually a problem rather quickly. Once the problem is identified, the believer is hooked on their drug of choice. Your choice is coffee. Coffee or drug of choice involves a routine to its inclusion. This routine satisfies the soul and may warm the spirit connection with Me as it does for you."

Oh, dear Jesus, help me. I know what You are asking me to do but the taste of coffee is a craving that is difficult to ignore.

"I am with you, My chosen one. I understand the weakness within you. Remember, I will never leave you nor forsake you."

What am I to do to overcome this?

"Be dependent on Me. Ask for My help and I will help you." (Matthew 7:7) *When you awake, surrender yourself to Me. Pray your special prayer as directed a few days ago - 'I awake today to praise You, Father. I awake today to serve You and Your Kingdom. I surrender to You wholly and completely. You are my God. I am yours.' Through your surrender comes surrender to Me and awareness. Often, you stumble to the kitchen to fix your coffee without thinking. Yet, this very act is what distracts you from My plan for wellness in your temple. Try a new approach and see how you respond."*

Beyond the curtain:

What is your weakness?

Pray: Oh, God, I am grateful for a new plan. Please help me to be steadfast. Come Spirit and give me strength.

Where can you post the awakening prayer?

"I awake today to praise You, Father. I awake today to serve You and Your Kingdom. I surrender to You wholly and completely. You are my God. I am Yours."

DAY 35: *"My chosen one, you are too busy."*

God, I am doing Your work and people need me.

"Oh, sweet one, listen to My words. You are only human. You are honored for the heart that you serve but you cannot endure this intensity without it affecting your well-being. Your well-being with Me will be affected. Do you want that?"

No! I cannot sacrifice my quiet time with You.

"Oh, but you have. You run about to do My work, but you do not run to Me. Your communion with Me is important to Me. I desire to commune with you. I want to hear you talk with Me and you listen to My words. This is the most important relationship you can cultivate. Without Me, your work for Me is nothing."

How do I find balance in the busyness of life?

"You prioritize what is important to you. If I am important to you then you will prioritize Me."

I am sorry, God. Please forgive me.

"When you prioritize time with Me, you are prioritizing time for yourself. By doing so, comfort and well-being is extended to you that cannot be explained. This happens through the power of the Holy Spirit and cannot be measured."

Father, show me how to prioritize my time. Show me where I am busy and what can be eliminated or reduced.

Beyond the curtain:

Meditate with the Holy Spirit. Ask for understanding of where you are too busy and how this can be changed.

What did you think of?

Where are you too busy?

How can you change your schedule to accommodate your personal well-being?

Pray: Lord, help me to make this change. Give me strength to change what I can to be in better health. Give me strength to overcome people's dissatisfaction with my choice. Pour into me Godly confidence, wisdom, discernment, and strength. Help me be bold. Thank You, Jesus. Amen.

DAY 36: God, I feel poorly today.

"Come to Me, My child, for you feel weary today. I will give you rest. I will hold you. I will give you all you need."

I do not feel like talking today.

"It is not necessary. Just rest in Me. Allow Me to nurture your soul and body."

(long pause with no words spoken)

"Where do you hurt?"

In my head and back.

"What do you need from Me?"

Can You soothe the pain?

"Yes. I was waiting for you to ask."

Lord, why do some people ask for healing and not receive it?

"Healing comes when the heart is ready."

What do You mean by ready?

"When the heart of the person seeking healing is fully surrendered to Me with acceptance of the outcome, no matter what, then the heart posture is positioned to receive from the fullness of My throne. One must trust and believe."

Beyond the curtain:

What in your body, soul, or spirit needs surrender to God?

Where do you strive (strive def: make great efforts to achieve or attain something; struggle or fight vigorously) that needs to surrender?

Pray: Lord, I surrender to You completely. Please help my heart posture to be fully surrendered to You and pleasing to You. Take my striving and calm my soul so I can surrender fully to Your plan. I honor You, God, with my entire being.

Affirmative Statement: I surrender _____ to God.
Post this statement in a location to remind yourself.

DAY 37: Lord, rain calms my soul. It is gentle and soothing. It gives me an excuse to curl up on the couch with You.

"Rain is meant to nourish the soil so growth may happen."

It feels as if it nourishes me. It brings calm into my spirit as I listen to the sound.

"Rain is a blessing from heaven to the earth. Without nourishment to the soul, one will wither and dry up."

How does one nourish their soul?

"Many people search for others to nourish their soul, but this is not true nourishment. True nourishment is when one sits in the presence of the Almighty and allows rain from heaven to sprinkle their soul. This nourishment resembles raindrops from heaven extended as birds chirping, quietness, warmth of the sun, sand between the toes, water on the body, smells that bring freshness, the taste of special treats, and unknown treasures that drift into one's existence."

It seems many are so busy with life that they miss this nourishment.

"Busyness is meant to distract and mislead one from the path of nourishment. I ask what are you forfeiting by ignoring what is yours? What are you teaching your children and family when you put busyness as the priority in your home? Do they not see what you do is what they, too, will do? Remember, My child, your actions teach others around you what they are to do."

Beyond the curtain:

Pray: Lord Jesus, open my eyes to see what I can change in my life so that I nourish my soul. Open my eyes to see what I can change to set a better example for my family. Amen.

Shut your eyes and meditate on the Spirit for 2 minutes.

What came to your mind?

If your mind was too busy to hear, then this is an indicator that your soul needs nourishing – your mind is too busy. Remind yourself of what is important in life. Is it happiness? Peace of mind? Accomplishing? Overcoming? Family? Putting yourself as a priority?
Thoughts:

What is important five years from now?

Ten years from now?

Twenty years from now?

I **WILL** take this action for my well-being and to nourish my soul:

DAY 38: *"Why is it important to serve Me faithfully while on this earth?"*

So that heaven may be brought to earth?

"Yes. That is partly accurate. It is true that the Good News be spread throughout the earth. It is true that My will is done through My people. Have you ever considered that I, the King of the Universe, desires a relationship with you?"

Wow. I was not expecting that answer.

"It brings Me great joy to commune with My people. I love to watch them grow and mature into who they are called to be. The joy it brings to Me explodes as fireworks on a summer day."

What gets in the way of that relationship developing?

"People get in their own way. They place expectations on themselves and on Me. Expectations is not how I operate. I am a fluid God who moves and breathes among His people. I must be fluid to commune with the different types of people."

What should we do to live outside expectations?

"Learn to get up every day in anticipation of what I will reveal to you. Anticipation brings excitement to the soul and curiosity builds. I will respond when someone embraces anticipation from Me."

Do we lack the ability to be curious with anticipation or has the world shut it down within us?

"Life's circumstances cause some people to never anticipate with curiosity because as children they learned that little comes from this anticipation. It is My hope to restore this curiosity and anticipation from Me, the one who made every person."

What is my role?

"Surrender and ask for anticipation, curiosity, and excitement to return to your soul."

Beyond the curtain:

Pray: Dear God, I want and desire anticipation, curiosity, and excitement in my soul. I surrender to You. I need Your help to recover this part of me that has been lost. Please hear my prayer and restore my soul. Thank You, Jesus, for hearing my prayer. Amen.

DAY 39: Lord, what frustrates You most?

"Religious works. People think they are religious when they do certain things. This has no part of Me. It is purely an act that desires conformity to an establishment of rules and regulations."

"Yes, this is a difficult topic."

Is religious a term You desire us use as believers in Christ?

"Religiosity stands for a set of rules enforced by a governing body. Faith in Jesus Christ is merely faith and is demonstrated through a relationship with Me. You are a follower of Jesus Christ."

Are people hindered in their relationship with You because of religious rules?

"Many people turn away from the faith due to rules placed upon them through religious establishments."

This is sad to me. What can we do to change this?

"Show My love to all people for you do not know what they have experienced in their life. I came to earth to show Myself to the world so they may see Truth not religion. Truth extends love and grace."

What about justice?

"I am a just God. I see all things, all motives, and actions. I extend love, grace, and justice. Justice is not My desire, but it is who I am. I must extend justice at given situations and circumstances."

How do we change our thinking that is wrapped around religious rules, obligation, guilt, shame, etc.?

"Seek Me. I am the one who can speak into these circumstances. Seek and you will find Me. Ask and it will be given."

Beyond the curtain:

Consider what you learned or assumed that needs correction and attention by God. Any ideas?

Pray: Dear God, thank You for loving me as much as You do. Thank You for caring that I am seen and heard by You. I lay before You those things I have learned or assumed is Your ways. I ask for You to speak into these areas, reveal what is inaccurate, and show me how to live by faith. If there are any ways within me that are not of faith and by religious means, then I ask that You reveal them to me. Thank You for loving me. I give You all praise, honor, and glory! Amen.

Other thoughts:

DAY 40: Father, are You with me?

"I am always with you. I will never leave you nor forsake you. You are Mine and I am yours."

Thank You so much. (pause)

I feel like You have not spoken to me. Did I do something?

"My child, communing with one another does not always require words. Did we not commune when you prepared your soil for planting? Did we not commune when you celebrated with your daughter? Did we not commune when you drove? Did we not commune when you made love with your husband? Did we not commune when you watch the birds and listen to their chirps? Of course, I was there!"

God, please forgive me.

"There is nothing to be forgiven. Recognize that I am in your midst always."

God, help me to recognize Your presence even if I cannot hear You.

Beyond the curtain:

Pray: God, remind me of ways You have been with me.

What came to mind:

Do you have a blank mind, and nothing came? If so, ask yourself these questions:

Do I have racing thoughts that prevent me from hearing from God? If so, consider sitting for a couple minutes to relax the mind. Find a meditation app that may be helpful or go to: https://drive.google.com/file/d/1kWTUbW7gfQzH8jVaLu7AWeLQ6ZGf2EHS/view?usp=sharing

Do I need to ask God to forgive me for something? If so, say this prayer: Dear God, I confess and repent of _____. I ask for Your forgiveness and healing. Give me strength to overcome this obstacle in my life. Thank You, Jesus. Amen.

Do I need to forgive myself or someone else for something? If so, say this prayer: Dear God, I forgive _____ for _____ (this can be difficult, but I have found to say it out loud repeatedly is the beginning of healing. Say it even if you cannot fully engage it. Remember, forgiveness is for **YOUR** healing **NOT** to validate someone's actions.)

After completing any of the above exercises,
Pray: God, remind me of ways You have been with me.

What came to mind:

DAY 41: God, what makes my space with You holy?

"My anointing is what you feel when you sit and do not want to leave. When you sit in this space and receive Me then this is holiness. When the space is unhindered – without distraction, this is a space conducive of holiness."

God, I realize this is easier for me because my life has slowed with no children at home and calmer routine than in the past. Many people have busy schedules and a busy home. How do these people establish this environment?

"Do you remember being young and having 'your corner' with a chair, pen, and pad? Do you remember getting up early to just sit with Me alone? Do you remember sharing Jesus with those whom you served? It is about the heart posture and intention."

What can get in the way of a good heart posture?

"Unforgiveness. Surrender. Hopelessness. Pride. Fear. Not seeking the best for your neighbor instead of yourself. Hate. Anger. Jealousy. Lack of love. Aggressiveness. Passivity."

(Pause and Ponder)

"It takes great boldness to live as a Christ follower."

How do we develop boldness?

"You cannot. I must live in you. It is only through Me that true boldness is purified in you."

Beyond the curtain:

Pray: Dear God, I want to have a heart posture to serve You. Show me what gets in the way for me.

What do you think gets in the way for you to have a good heart posture?

Pray: Dear God, I confess and repent that I have agreed with _____ (from above). Please forgive me and help me to overcome this. Come live inside me so I may be bold. Give me what I need. In Jesus, I pray. Amen.

DAY 42: God, it seems most people struggle with something. Is that true?

"Humanity is wired to want more, achieve more, and succeed. For Christ followers, it is imperative for each to remain connected with Me. When a person is focused on wanting, achieving, and succeeding then this often distracts from their relationship with Me. Connectedness to Me often comes through struggle because a person will recognize they need Me, someone greater than themselves. Struggle varies from person to person. When a person's struggle draws them closer to Me, they will see their struggle disappear and My power illuminated. Dependence upon Me is of greatest importance."

It seems Americanized ways eliminate the need for support or community among Christ followers. This brings concern to me given Scripture re-enforces the gathering of God's people (Hebrews 10:24-25, Romans 12:4-5, Acts 2:46-47, etc.).

"It is said where two or three 'gather together' so am I there. It is important that My people 'gather together' through prayer, celebration, and communion. The formality of the gathering is not important."

Beyond the curtain:

What do you yearn for?

Where do you struggle?

Consider where your dependence needs shifting from yourself to dependence on God. What can you "let go of" and begin to depend on God for?

Pray: Dear God, I confess and repent that I try to handle life's circumstances myself. I need Your help. I lay down this yearning for _____ and ask that You give me contentment and awareness of what I need. I need Your help with my struggle of _____.

Please help me. I surrender to You completely. Open my eyes to see and my ears to hear from You. Thank You, Jesus. Amen.

Who can you ask for prayer or to seek as a Christ follower in your life?

If you do not have a community of Christ followers, consider who or where that may be. Thoughts?

Pray: God, I need other Christ followers in my life. I need community to walk and laugh with. Please send me those people. Show me where to go, who is safe, and walks authentically with You. Thank You, God. Amen.

Notes:

DAY 43: What does community look like?

"Community is a group of people who serve Me. Their walk with Me may vary yet they are willing to learn from one another. They are open to correction and celebration. They commune in spirit, soul, and body where their spirits engage Mine with their spiritual gifts revealed. Their soul or identity is healed and refined to their God-given calling so they may fulfill the Great Commission. Their bodies serve as a temple of the Holy Spirit and strive for purity. Surrender and unity embody the community. Togetherness is inclusive to all who wish to belong."

Wow! God, is there such a place that I can belong?

"Many yearn for this type of community, but few have it. For those who seek, you will find. For those who yearn, it will be given. For those who establish, it will be offered. Seek Me for these things and I will direct your steps."

This makes me want to start a community of Christ followers who yearn for this too.

"If it is My desire, it will happen."

God, how do we change the trajectory of the church or body of Christ in America?

"It is changing even now. Fret not, My Chosen One. The Great Awakening will grow the church as never before. Be prepared for the body of Christ to operate unlike times past for it will expand and unify under My authority and power."

Beyond the curtain:

Read about the Great Commission in Matthew 28:16-20.

What are your top 3 strengths?
1. _____
2. _____
3. _____

Which of these strengths come the easiest to you?

Often what comes the easiest is how we are gifted to share with others. Consider how you may extend this to others.

Pray: Dear God, thank You for equipping me with these strengths. Open my eyes to see how I can use them for You and Your people. I give You all praise, honor, and glory! Amen.

How can you use your strengths to help others?

What can you do to join in God's movement in America, in the world?

DAY 44: Lord, what do You desire from me today?

"Sweet one, to commune with Me is lovely, to serve Me in your chosen way is radical, and to fulfil the Great Commission on earth as desired in heaven comes with great reward."

What does the Great Commission look like for this day and age?

> **The Great Commission – Matthew 28:16-20**
> But the eleven disciples proceeded to Galilee, to the mountain which Jesus had designated to them. And when they saw Him, they worshiped *Him*; but some were doubtful. And Jesus came up and spoke to them, saying, "All authority in heaven and on earth has been given to Me. Go, therefore, and make disciples of all the nations, baptizing them in the name of the Father and the Son and the Holy Spirit, teaching them to follow all that I commanded you; and behold, I am with you always, to the end of the age."

"My child, My child, do not fret for I am with you always. Follow the lead of My spirit to guide you. Some are gifted in evangelism, others in discipling, while others are teachers. Do not fret, My child, for wherever you are passionate, the gift I've given you is where I will meet you."

It seems distractions happen to take us away from Your perfect will.

"Yes, this is true. Distractions will mislead but the road is always brought in alignment with My plan. Never fear for I will lead each back onto the path that leads to hope. Seek Me and you will find. Ask and it will be given."

We thank You, Father, for this assurance.

Beyond the curtain:

Do you know your gifting - apostle, prophet, evangelist, pastor, teacher?

If not, you can take the free test here: https://fivefoldministry.com/static/learn-about-the-five-fold-ministry

Do you find yourself stuck in fear, lack (I'm not good enough), or ego (shame or pride)? These areas can hold you back from accomplishing God's perfect will in your life. If you see that one or more of these areas have a hold on you, say this prayer:

Dear God, I confess and repent that I agreed with (fear, lack, or ego) and the impact it has had on my life. I repent of this decision, and I ask for Your forgiveness and healing. From my spirit alive in Christ, I revoke this agreement with (fear, lack, or ego). I place these entities in the heavenly courts and ask that You sentence them on my behalf. I ask that You give me healing to go where You want me to go. Protect me, my bloodline, and my sphere of influence as I go through this journey. Thank You, Jesus! Amen.

What do you need to ask of God? He says ask and it will be given (Matthew 7:7; Luke 11:9).

Prayer has no need to be fancy. Just ask in your language!

Notes:

DAY 45: Oh, God, I feel I have not connected with You for the past few days, and I have not heard from You.

"My beautiful one, communion with Me is not contained. It is to be shared. That is what you have done. You shared your communion with a friend."

I have much to learn about communion with You.

"Learning is always present when your heart desires more from Me. Rest in communion with Me with no pressure to achieve or guilt from not connecting."

Ahhhh ... (deep breath and shoulders relaxed)

"Just sitting with Me, connecting with My creation such as the birds of the air, and the sounds. The connectedness with yourself in your environment brings true joy to My heart. There is great communion between yourself and your environment. Allow yourself a moment to just sit and receive."

Long pause to connect ...

"When you give of yourself to others there is a blessing that is given but be reminded you must reconnect to be replenished. Both are good and perfect."

I give You all praise, honor, and glory!

Beyond the curtain:

Consider Jesus' actions in these stories for they represent examples of how we are to give to others but also care for ourselves, as Jesus did, by retreating for a time of replenishment.

Read Mark 4-8, Luke 8

Where have you given of yourself to others but not replenished yourself?

What can you do to replenish yourself amidst difficult life circumstances?
    30 minutes replenishment ideas:

    Half-a-day replenishment ideas:

    Full day replenishment ideas:

What plans need to be made to allow the above to happen?

Pray: Lord, I need Your help. I need time to be restored. Please provide what I need for this to happen. Thank You and I give You praise. Amen.

DAY 46: God, my anxiety and tension has increased.

"I see. Did you ask Me for help?"

Ummmm ... I don't think I did for this problem.

"No, you didn't."

"I always desire to help no matter how large or small the matter. Did you ask at one moment and I gave insight? Yes, I did. I can resolve problems. Trust Me."

I am sorry. Please forgive me.

"You are forgiven. The anxiety you place upon yourself is unwarranted."

Lord, I am so very tired.

"This is because you are striving to accomplish that which is unnecessary. Ask and it will be given. Next time, remember to ask and I will help."

Deep breath. Relaxed shoulders. Finding my calm place.

Thank You, Father.

Beyond the curtain:

Ponder how often you ask the Lord to help you amidst projects or problems. Thoughts:

Where do you think you place the most pressure on yourself that could be alleviated if you asked God to help?

Pray: Lord, I confess that I try to handle situations by myself. I ask for Your forgiveness. Help me to see a new way to engage You and to recognize that You desire to help me. I ask for Your anointing to fall upon me. Open my eyes to see and ears to hear what You desire. Thank You, Jesus. Amen.

DAY 47: *"Do you realize how important you are in this world?"*

Not really.

"Without you, people would not engage the power of Christ in their life. Many wander as if lost. They do not seek because no one shows them. They do not hear because they have no one to show them how to hear. People flounder because they are not taught how to live with Me."

Lord, is this pertinent to all people?

"This statement is true for all. All true worshippers affect those around them in some way – good or bad."

I am reminded of the gospel where Jesus commands all to go and make disciples (Matthew 28:19).

"Yes, the greatest commandment is to love as Christ loved and seek Me with all your heart, mind, soul, and strength." (Matthew 22:36-40)

Lord, how do we remain focused on these objectives and not our day-to-day issues?

"The ONLY way is to remain connected to Me. Connectedness overrides anxiety, fear, pride, and a host of emotions that will attempt to derail you from My perfect will for you and for those in your life. When you remain connected then you are nourished and fed with unexplainable heavenly food. The value is so great that there is no match on this earth to fill it in the same way."

Oh, Lord, help me to always be in the sweet spot of connectedness with You. I am desperate to not lose it and to share it with others. It is lovely to me.

"Ask and it will be given."

Beyond the curtain:

Consider a tree with its root deep into the soil, the roots are many, going various directions. Some of the roots are large, others are small but there are many. These roots nourish the tree.

What are the "roots" in your life that bring nourishment to your soul?

1. _____
2. _____
3. _____
4. _____
5. _____
6. _____

If you are having a hard time identifying the roots, consider where you go to when you need something (God, Scripture, hometown, beach, mountains, or people). Consider something you had in the past but possibly forgot how important it is to you (ex: fishing, painting, sunrise, kayaking, music, etc.).

Plan to nourish your soul through YOUR root system!
My Plan:

1. _____
2. _____
3. _____
4. _____

Notes:

DAY 48: God, why do we physically hurt? It seems to hinder my endurance for the Kingdom of God.

"Pain is not My desire for you. It is used by Me to bring you closer to Me and more dependent upon Me. I am with you always."

I feel poorly.

"I know. Be reminded that I am with you. I will bring fullness of life to you and for all who seek Me. You are My chosen one. You are here on this earth to fulfill the greatest commandment. Through this charge, you will spread the gospel of Christ to those who need Me most while you develop an intimate relationship with Me. Do not forsake this command."

Matthew 22:37-39 Jesus replied, "Love the Lord your God with all your heart and with all your soul and with all your mind. This is the first and greatest commandment. And the second is like it: Love your neighbor as yourself."

God, I surrender to You wholly and completely. I pray for endurance while I am on earth.

"You will endure until the time has come for you to exit this earth. Accomplish My will until your last breath. And, yes, My will is My greatest commandment for all people."

Can all people love You?

"Yes. Many people neglect Me. They seek fulfillment in other ways neglecting Me in the moment. They overlook My role in nature, connections with people, and the tiny, bizarre moments that transpire in everyday life. People are too busy and overlook the obvious. If people would sit and engage their quiet space, they would recognize Me and the move of My Spirit among them."

(take a few minutes to sit, relax, and focus on your space)

God, there is an anxious intensity in me.

"Yes, it is a pressure you place on yourself to accomplish. It is My desire you 'just be.'"

What am I to do from this point?

"Stretch, breathe, and remind yourself you have no requirements from Me. Learn to meditate amongst demands."

Lord, help me to relax in order to fulfil Your will through me.

Beyond the curtain:

How do you neglect God in your everyday moments?

What strategy can you incorporate into your everyday moments to bring peace within yourself AND accomplish God's plan for your life?   (unplug from phone/social media? Meditation? Gardening? Fishing? Drawing? Journaling?)

Pray: God, I ask for Your help. I need You, Jesus, and Holy Spirit. I need You to show me HOW to overcome anxiousness, guilt, and pressures I place upon myself. I surrender to You wholly and completely. Amen.

DAY 49: *"Consider your actions, My Chosen one, both today and in the past. What actions of yours are unworthy of My standards? Consider Proverbs 6: 16-19, 'There are six things the Lord hates – no, seven things he detests, haughty eyes, a lying tongue, hands that kill the innocent, a heart that plots evil, feet that race to do wrong, a false witness who pours out lies, a person who sows discord in a family.' (NLT) Chosen one, which of these linger in your soul that cause you harm?"*

Oh God, I do not want to consider that You hate things I have done. Please do not ask me to consider these.

"In order for you to remain beyond the curtain, this step must be taken. Do you desire this relationship of intimacy with Me?"

Yes! Oh, yes!

"Then choose which of these seven things you have chosen."

(pause with reflection)

Oh, God, I ask Your forgiveness for my actions. Please forgive me.

"You are forgiven."

Am I forgiven? Am I not held accountable for my actions?

"You are forgiven. This is the power of relationship with Me. To cultivate this relationship with Me allows for communion beyond comprehension and joy as tall as mountains."

Oh, how I praise You, Father God, Lord Jesus, and Holy Spirit!

Beyond the curtain:
Consider Proverbs 6, identify which of these is brought to your attention.

1. Haughty eyes
2. Lying tongue
3. Hands that kill the innocent
4. Heart that plots evil
5. Feet that race to do wrong
6. False witness who pours out lies
7. Person who sows discord in a family

Pray: Dear God, I confess and repent of _____.
Please forgive me.

Remind yourself you are forgiven. As Jesus said, "Neither do I (condemn you). Go and sin no more." (John 8: 1-11)

Pray: Dear God, thank You for forgiving me. I am grateful. Show me how to live differently. I give Jesus all praise, honor, and glory. Amen.

Notes:

DAY 50: God, what is Your heart for humanity?

"To love one another, depend on Me for I am God, and share the gospel of Christ for all to see."

Which of these is most important?

"One cannot hold more value than another for without one of these the others cannot be fulfilled."

If someone considers one of these a point to start, where should they begin?

"Love one another is the greatest commandment. For this reason, one should love others as they love themselves."

How do we love difficult or bad people?

"Have you ever had difficult times in your life?"

Yes.

"It is with other people, too, for each person's journey presents obstacles that cause discontentment or heartache. Be reminded of these things when you encounter those difficult people."

Lord, help me to love well, surrender to You fully, and share Jesus through words and actions.

Beyond the curtain:

When considering God's heart for you, what is the area you desire to focus more intently?

1. Love others
2. More dependence on God
3. Share the gospel of Jesus

How can you love others better?

How can you depend on God more?

How can you share the gospel of Jesus Christ?

DAY 51: God, our society breeds success through money and fame. How are we to live amidst these standards?

"Every society has challenges and hurdles to navigate. Some societies have limited food, electricity, and water. Their challenges present dependence on Me for their daily needs. Are not your requirements the same? Society says to achieve and do independent of others, but I say depend on Me for your needs. You are trying to meet your needs among these demands. Your needs are different but, yet the same. Your daily need may be contrary to popular belief such as quiet, contentment, and living within your means. These remain vital to humanity."

Are You saying both societies have a lack of necessities?

"Yes. Both require basic needs. One is forced to live within their means, searching to meet their basic needs while the other is forced to release beyond their means to meet their necessity."

Adaptation seems evident to me. To some degree we have adapted to our environment but without dependence on You, the striving is present no matter the culture.

"Yes, striving is the opposite of dependence."

Lord, help me not to strive for anything but first to begin with dependence on You for all things.

Beyond the curtain:

Definition of striving: make great efforts to achieve or gain something; struggle or fight vigorously. (Oxford Dictionary)

Where do you strive in your life?

What is within you that causes this striving? To attain? To accomplish? To overcome?

Do you feel you depend on God as you seek to attain, accomplish, or overcome?

Read **Philippians 1:20-24** (NLT), Paul states, "For I fully expect and hope that I will never be ashamed, but that I will continue to be bold for Christ, as I have been in the past. And I trust that my life will bring honor to Christ, whether I live or die. For to me, living means living for Christ, and dying is even better. But if I live, I can do more fruitful work for Christ. So, I really don't know which is better. I'm torn between two desires: I long to go and be with Christ, which would be far better for me. But for your sakes, it is better that I continue to live."

Phil. 2:3-5, "Don't be selfish; don't try to impress others. Be humble, thinking of others as better than yourselves. Don't look out only for your own interests, but take an interest in others, too. You must have the same attitude that Christ Jesus had."

Phil. 3:12-14, "I don't mean to say that I have already achieved these things or that I have already reached perfection. But I press on to possess that perfection for which Christ Jesus first possessed me. No, dear brothers and sisters, I have not achieved it, but I focus on this one thing: Forgetting the past and looking forward to what lies ahead. I press on to reach the end of the race and receive the heavenly prize for which God, through Christ Jesus, is calling us."

How can you attain, accomplish, or overcome **AND** depend on God for this desire?

Pray: Dear God, I surrender to You fully in all my desires to attain, accomplish, and overcome. I want my desires to be Your desires. Align my heart with Your heart. Orchestrate a mighty move in my life to be who You have called me to be. I give You all praise, honor, and glory! Amen.

DAY 52: God, sometimes it seems You do not speak or are not present.

"Yes, that may be the way you feel about the situation, but I am always with you."

Why does it feel this way?

"In order for Me to help you understand how I created you; you must know what it is like to have Me always, at limited moments, or to experience nothing. Why, you ask? Because I desire you to always rest in Me whether you hear Me or experience Me with contentment and security of knowing I am always present. Yes, those who have experienced insecurity with parental figures will struggle with Me at times. However, I am always with them, no matter what they may feel. They must look for the moments that affirm My presence. I will show them."

What are some examples of how You reveal Your presence with people?

"Reassurance comes in various ways. Some through numbers whether it is multiples of a number or three experiences that affirm My direction. Another person may find dimes at random moments signifying My presence with them. Others may see sequential numbers that are only between them and Myself. Others may see a specific bird to signify My presence with them while others may see reoccurring shapes. These represent My communication with My people. It is specific to My people and unlimited in possibilities."

How will a person know it is You?

"Often the reoccurrence happens repeatedly until the person recognizes it is special. This brings great joy to My heart when the person recognizes it is Me."

Beyond the curtain:

How does God speak to you? In words? In symbols? In numbers?

If you are uncertain, ask God to reveal himself to you in this way. Pray: Dear God, I know You are present with me. Forgive me for doubting. I want to experience You in a deeper way. I ask that You shower me with random moments of Your presence. I ask that there is no deception to mislead me but only You and Your Holy Spirit. Thank You, God. Amen.

Notes:

DAY 53: God, the Apostle Paul wrote in Ephesians 5:22-23 (NASB), that "Wives, *subject yourselves* to your own husbands, as to the Lord." In other versions, it says for the woman to submit. Lord, this causes significant problems for women in our culture. What do You say? Lord, please do not let me and my thoughts stand in the way of what You say.

"My teacher of the Word, the Apostle Paul was of great value in the culture in his day. The culture of the gentiles was encouraged to follow the Jewish traditions. In Jewish tradition, the women are subject to men. However, as a gentile in America, your culture is quite different. My child, you as a woman are created by Me and called by Me. A man is created by Me and called by Me. When a man and a woman come together under My authority and called by Me then they are living as I created them. They are to submit to Me first then all things will be given. It is not my desire for the man to lord over the woman nor the woman to be subservient to the man. This does not align with Jesus' teaching evident in the gospels. Jesus instructed all to come to Him and be saved. Submission to one another is the desire of the father."

What do I say to those who live according to Ephesians?

"Does obedience to the Word not bring honor? Yes, of course! Those who honor My Word will be honored. Their misunderstanding is not considered when obedience is at the heart of the understanding."

Thank You, God. What would Jesus say to the Gentiles in America today given the same topic?

"Love one another as I have loved the church. For My people, called by My name, are lovely in My eyes. Love one another in this way and there is no oppression from husband nor the wife. Live in love, obedience, and surrender to one another. This will create great joy in your hearts. This will present an example to others worthy of your calling."

Thank You, Jesus, Father God, and Holy Spirit. I am grateful for Your words.

Beyond the curtain:

What part of this day's devotional challenges you? Upsets you? Or gives you encouragement?

Consider the root of your emotional response to this devotional. Is it anger, frustration, sadness, joy, determination, etc. What emotions are you feeling?

1. _____
2. _____
3. _____

Do your emotions stem from the teaching you have received, toward a person, God?

To whom can you talk about this if so desired?

Thoughts of your next step for this topic?

DAY 54: *"Who are you?"*

I feel like some days I am that person who has all the contentment and peace needed for life. Other days, I feel as if, what am I doing on this earth? Where am I going? Am I doing all I need to do to survive? Have I done wrong that needs re-written?

"You are My child in whom I am greatly pleased. You evaluate yourself with determination to fix the brokenness. You go and search and follow Me with a whole heart of surrender. You, My child, are human. Your humanness cannot be changed except through the power of the Holy Spirit as you connect with Me. I know this is your heart's desire. Continue to follow Me with an open heart with full surrender. I will direct your steps and you will go where I have planned for you. Fret not over wrongs. Fret not over the rights. There is no fretting for those who serve Me, only peace."

How do we keep balance between perfectionism and apathy?

"Perfectionism brings stress and apathy brings unwillingness. Balance is freedom. Freedom in the Spirit has no human stress and includes promptings in the spirit that create balance negating apathy. Freedom to soar. Freedom to be. Freedom to go. Freedom to be who I created you to be."

What stands in the way of us being who You created us to be?

"Who you think you should be."

Beyond the curtain:

What does freedom look like to you?

What pressure do you put on yourself that you THINK you should be or do?

What is one thing you can do for yourself to remove this pressure?

DAY 55: Why are some people more competitive than others?

"People are created to endure. Some are more resilient while others have less intensity to succeed."

Is one better than another?

"Is it not true that while one person seeks attainment, another seeks contentment? While this may be true now, their roles may reverse at another time in life. Life presents timing of each at different stages for each person. The goal for each person is to join in the journey of where I am leading that person."

How do we know where You are taking us?

"Often you may not know. Often the uncertainty is greater than the certainty. However, I seek to reveal Myself to My people if My people desire to know Me. One must seek Me, and you will find Me. Ask and it will be given. Wisdom is given without stipulation. So, ask."

Why are we stubborn and not seek Your help?

"Humanity is wired to achieve, accomplish, and overcome. Many believe they can do this without My help. This is where I am the greatest – to reveal myself in undeniable ways. Just ask."

Beyond the curtain:

Where do you seek to achieve, accomplish, or overcome WITHOUT asking God to help?

Read Romans 13:3, "because of the privilege and authority God has given me, I give each of you this warning. Don't think you are better than you really are. Be honest in your evaluation of yourselves, measuring yourselves by the faith God has given us" NLT.

If you continue to read, the chapter talks about the body of Christ and how we are different. Through this difference, we are to love and care for one another with no revenge.

What part of this chapter in Romans catches your attention and why?

Where do you want to invite God into your desires to achieve? Work, finances, wants, or needs?

Do you struggle to invite God into your deepest yearnings or desires? If so, ask yourself what makes you think He does not want to be a part of this intimate place. Thoughts?

Pray: I confess and repent that I neglect You in my deepest desires. Please forgive me for this decision. Help me, Father, to sit before You without hesitation and concern, for I know Your ways are best and perfect for me. I surrender to You completely. I ask that You open my eyes to see and ears to hear all that You have for me. Thank You, Jesus. Amen.

DAY 56: God, it seems so hard to connect with You sometimes.

"That does not mean I am not here."

I feel You but I do not hear You.

"Do friends sit together sometimes without talking?"

Yes.

"Then we are friends. Don't let your expectations disrupt what you do have."

(long pause taking in my environment)

"What do you have?"

Quiet, calm, a peaceful existence, birds chirping, Your presence, and all that I need.

"Do not forget what you have. It is a gift."

Beyond the curtain:

Do you find it hard to connect with God, hear His voice, or see Him moving? If so, please consider yourself normal. I have sat with many people to hear from God and each person hears differently. Some people see or hear things, others have feelings, while others get nothing. Do not fret over *YOUR* style of connecting with God. Whatever your style looks like it is perfect because that is the way God made you and it is for a reason and purpose.

How do you hear from God?
- Visual
- Hearing
- Feeling
- Smelling
- Other

What are some examples of when you have heard from God?

What expectations have you placed on yourself and God that may be distracting you from what you do have?

Take a moment and list what you do have:

Pray: Thank You, God, for always being present with me. Thank You for what I have. Show me how to recognize how You speak to me. I praise You, Jesus! Amen.

DAY 57: *"This is the day that the LORD has made; let us rejoice and be glad in it."* Psalm 118:24

How are we to rejoice, God?

"What is the definition of rejoicing?"

Oxford dictionary says to feel or show great joy or delight.

"The heart can show great joy and delight without a forced external display."

Lord, how can we grow our joy and delight?

"The more a person places effort on joy, the easier it becomes to be delightful. If one focuses on joyful things, then this is what they will see. If one focuses on negative matters, then their joy and delight diminishes."

It seems some people focus on the negative and it is hard to live among them.

"Maybe, but is it not true that I send you to those people so you can bring joy to their hearts?"

Okay. I see that. How can I stay positively focused among the negativities?

"These people have ideas to consider, too. Share with them and receive what they have then both will benefit. Connectedness with Me is always the answer."

Beyond the curtain:

How can you get outside yourself today and share with someone?

Who in your life needs a text or call from you?

Do you feel great joy or delight in your spirit or soul? _____
If so, how are you feeling it?

If you do not feel great joy or delight, is there something you are waiting on?

Do you feel numbed out? Often, lack of joy may result from life's experiences. I am sorry if you have experienced bad things in life. I know this is not God's desire for you. Remind yourself how strong you are to have gone through these things. Remind yourself you are resilient and an overcomer. With God, you are stronger than if you were alone.

Read Psalm 46.

> God is our refuge and strength,
>   always ready to help in times of trouble.
> So we will not fear when earthquakes come
>   and the mountains crumble into the sea.
> Let the oceans roar and foam.
>   Let the mountains tremble as the waters surge!
> Be still, and know that I am God!
>   I will be honored by every nation.
>   I will be honored throughout the world.
> The LORD of Heaven's Armies is here among us;
>   the God of Israel is our fortress.

I encourage you to fight to have quiet with the LORD. This is your strength and wisdom! Fight for it!

DAY 58: *"Today is a new day. The dawn breaks with newness to spread throughout the earth. Even as those who seek to destroy cannot get a footing because I am God, and I am in control. Those who seek to join Me in this new day are welcome. Come to Me all who are weary, and I will give you rest beyond measure. Join Me and see that it is good. Join Me and feel refreshed in your soul. Join Me and you will see new things, new joys, and new victories. Come to the water, come to Me. Come and be refreshed."*

Why is today new and different than yesterday?

"Because I am God, I am pouring upon My people, a dose of awakening so each may go forth where mountains will move when they speak."

It sounds as if You are putting an army together.

"You are correct. My end time army. An army that cannot be held down nor defeated."

What is our role?

"Surrender to Me. Surrender all that you have both in action and word. I will honor you as you take this step."

I am not sure people fully understand how to surrender, God.

"You are correct. Many find themselves apathetic to the motion."

Is there a model in which You can share?

"Yes. Sit, kneel, or lay quietly. Repeat these words: I surrender my mind, body, spirit, and soul to You fully. I pray that absolutely nothing will interfere or invade the space where You and I connect. I ask You to reveal to me what I am to know, think, or feel. Awaken me to Your presence and the plans You have for me. Help me to experience You in Your fullness and understanding. I am wholly Yours. Jesus, Father God, and Holy Spirit, I give You all praise, honor, and glory. Amen."

How often should we say these words?

"Daily."

Beyond the curtain:

Do you have reservation to take this action? If so, write it down.

If you desire to repeat the surrender prayer as above, but stated some reservation, pray this first:
Dear God, I admit that I have reservations of _____.
I repent of this struggle, and I ask for Your help.

Pray: I surrender my mind, body, spirit, and soul to You fully. I pray that absolutely nothing will interfere or invade the space where You and I connect. I ask You to reveal to me what I am to know, think, or feel. Awaken me to Your presence and the plans You have for me. Help me to experience You in Your fullness and understanding. I am wholly Yours. Jesus, Father God, and Holy Spirit, I give You all praise, honor, and glory.

Notes:

DAY 59: What do You expect from us, God?

"Expectations are demands. That is not who I am. I desire communion with My people not outlandish behaviors that do not connect us."

Okay, what do You desire from us?

"My desire is that My people will awake every day to first, sit with Me to hear My voice. Second, as I speak to My people, often there is something to act upon. This may be outside of oneself or an act within oneself. Third, more than anything, it is My desire to see My people follow through with the action. This brings greater communion between them and Me."

Do expectations get us in trouble with You and people?

"Expectations are a way humanity desires to control their situation. Expectations can get out of control and cause great dysfunction in relationships. It is My desire that kindness and love be given to others in your life not expectations."

How do we lay down our expectations?

"Just as you surrender to Me, so you surrender expectations and demands upon others. Give yourself and others the freedom to be who they are not what you expect of them or of yourself."

Beyond the curtain:

What do you prefer to focus on for today's message from God?

Read Matthew 5:1-12.

Which beatitude stands out to you?

Pray: God, in the beatitudes You say, You bless those who _____.
Help me to _____. I receive Your blessings. Thank You!
Amen.

DAY 60: *"Be grateful for what you have. Grateful for health, both in the mind and body, as well as spirit. Gratefulness for resilience to overcome life's obstacles, abilities to survive, and that you understand how to navigate life's challenges."*

Why do we (humanity) want what we do not have?

"Contentment. Contentment drives a person to do or want things they do not have. A person believes IF they get what they do not have then they will be content. This is a false narrative. Contentment, when embraced in all circumstances, brings one into a position of acceptance and understanding of their position."

If contentment is accepted, then what happens after understanding? How is contentment produced from understanding?

"Given specific circumstances to include depression and anxiety, and a person will gain understanding from which they have prayed and sought My direction, then this understanding produces insight and the motivation to change their situation. It is discontentment of material belongings and money that sidetracks humanity."

Beyond the curtain:

Where do you find yourself discontent in life?

What part of your life needs acceptance?

What part of your life needs insight from God?

Pray: God, I need Your help. I surrender to You.
I present to You this situation of need:

I am asking for insight and wisdom about:

Show me what to do next and the motivation needed to pursue this change. Thank You for hearing my prayer.

Apply one of these verses to the part of your life needing acceptance. Post it somewhere as a reminder.

Psalm 34:18
The Lord is near to the brokenhearted and saves the crushed in spirit.

Psalm 37:23
The Lord directs the steps of the godly. He delights in every detail of their lives.

Proverbs 20:15
Wise words are more valuable than much gold and many rubies.

Three words to take away from today's devo:

    1.
    2.
    3.

DAY 61: *"Today is the day the LORD has made. Let us rejoice and be glad in it. Thus, saith the LORD."*

How are we to rejoice?

"Let your heart be light over daily matters for I am with you. I will supply all your needs."

I think many people worry and fret too much.

"Yes, have I not supplied for the birds of the air? Have I not made the worms and fish, both in earth and sea? Yes! Yes! Yes! To commune with Me is to sit in the secret place, no matter the time nor location, and listen to My voice. Yes, My voice is revealed differently for all people, but I am always present for all people. Fretting will not add one hour to your life, My chosen people. Learn to enjoy and rejoice in the small births of life."

God, I understand we are tempted to embrace fear, lack, shame, or pride. These produce worry, fretting, and anxiety throughout our lifetime. I understand that we must confess and repent of these. However, what is it that we can do that is pivotal to take us beyond the repentance and into the rejoicing?

"My chosen one, freedom in the spirit to accept forgiveness leads to rejoicing. Is it not true that when one confesses that you often lack forgiveness of oneself? Do you not place pressure upon yourself to move beyond it yet with irony you place the anxiety upon yourself once again? Thus, learn to release yourself and rejoice in the freedom."

Thank You, Father.

Beyond the curtain:

Where do you worry and fret too much (fear, lack, shame, or pride)?

Pray: I confess and repent with the agreement of fear, worry, lack, shame, and/or pride and the impact it has had on my life (worry/fret/anxiety). I ask for Your forgiveness and healing. Help me to live in freedom and move beyond holding myself to an unrealistic standard. I release myself. Amen.

It may be hard to believe that God wants you to live in freedom. His freedom coexists with the Holy Spirit and brings you into rejoicing. Allow yourself this opportunity to go here. Begin to assess what theological teachings place expectations that drive you to perfectionism. Often, these teachings are misunderstood in the Scripture. Perfectionism is a culprit of worry and anxiety.

Sit in your sacred place and see yourself handing perfectionism to Jesus. Allow His voice to speak louder than your own as well as others in your life.

Thoughts:

DAY 62: The sea is vast in its magnificence. There are both calm and power, beauty and pain, understanding and questions, as well as past, present, and future. It seems You draw many to the sea for multiple reasons. What is it about the sea that brings healing to a person?

"Humanity opens their exploration of self when they sit at water's edge. This exploration allows healing to embody the soul and step beyond oneself into stark awareness of oneself. When a soul interacts with their circumstances coupled with the power of undeniable strength and beauty, one will assess, gather, and process anguish and love within themselves. However, one must allow themselves to touch the deep places that may cause pain. When this is allowed, the pain will be touched by Me."

My first thought begs the question, will the pain go away, but this feels like a human yearning. Instead, I have an image of Your hand touching the pain within.

"Humanity is wired to gather what brings shelter, safety, and calm. Do the birds of the air do the same? Yes! One moment they gather food to eat while the next moment they enjoy their nest to rejuvenate. How is humanity any different? Do the birds of the air flock together? Yes! Even those with different markings cohabitate to share life."

How are we different than the birds of the air?

"You are not. Yes, you have a soul but all you need can be learned from the birds of the air."

Beyond the curtain:

When you consider your needs and the future, what or where begs your attention and communion with the Father so you may heal and grow?

Give yourself a deadline to follow through with this plan – date:

Where:

Goal of the event:

People to take or not:

Things to do during this healing event:
- _____
- _____
- _____
- _____
- _____

Other thoughts:

SECTION II

The next portion of this devotional is intended to transition the reader to dependence upon the Spirit and less dependence upon the writer for thought provoking conversation with the Father. As you read, take what you have learned in the first portion of the devotional to begin asking your questions of God as well as yourself.

I encourage you to obtain a journal or notebook. Begin by writing the date at the top of the page. Making notes of what you are thinking, as well as location, can be important. Then, as you read and pray, God will give you thoughts. Write these thoughts in your journal. Remember, there may be days or weeks that He may not speak AND that is okay.

Find a location to store your journals when they are full. I have found it is helpful to write the start and end dates of the journal on the outside of the journal with a marker. This may be useful if you need to return to your journal.

Remember, this process is yours. It is between you and God, no one else. This is your private information. Store it accordingly. You are God's chosen instrument for what He is calling you to do. There is no one else like you. God has special plans for you because you are uniquely made. There is no need to be perfect in this journey. God is our perfection and more reason to remain connected to Him. Relax and enjoy the journey before you!

DAY 63: Pray: Lord Jesus, I come to You today. I need You. I ask for wisdom and discernment. Send all I need. God, what do You want to say today?

"My chosen one, life's journey is for humanity to engage. I made humanity so you might have the freedom to experience life before heavenly rewards. The spirit is the same whether on earth or heaven, but the soul and body are earthly necessities. Yes! Yes, the only way to survive the earth and its demands are to be in tune with My spirit. This is accomplished by learning to engage your spirit and the relationship between us. This is how you are made strong. This is the power humanity desires on earth. This will make you great in the Kingdom of God. Do not forsake this connection with Me. Do not give up. Do not underestimate what this connection can do for you."

Lord, I never want to leave this space of connectedness.

"I understand. One day you will never leave it but while you are on earth your goal is to spread the Good News to all. Humanity is confused and misled. Humanity is fearful, hopeless, and in disarray. My people, called by My name, must advance the Kingdom of God to all in their sphere. I will open doors and I will close doors. I will provide and I will remove. This is all for your benefit, My children. Do not hesitate, for when I am with you nothing, absolutely nothing, can interfere."

Scripture for the day: I Corinthians 2
Beyond the curtain: Get your notebook. Listen to the voice of God's Spirit. Begin writing what the Spirit says.

Notes:

DAY 64: Pray: Lord Jesus, I come to You today. I need You. I ask for wisdom and discernment. Send all I need.

"Speak Truth today."

What do You desire I speak of today?

"Just as the sea has salt so do you, My children, have salt. Do not lose your saltiness! I made you to dispense your saltiness for you will be replenished. Do not forsake doing this good for others. Have not others invested in you? Yes! You are to invest yourself in others to pass on the salt of the Lord for all to see. What is saltiness? Saltiness is a preservative that preserves humanity. Many cannot see but without salt, humanity would wither and die. It is the job of every human to baste themselves in the saltiness from above and pass along this preservative to others."

God, it seems humanity is full of lustful desires and our world is changing drastically for those lusts.

"It is true, My chosen one. It is true. Unlike any other time in the world, humanity is self-focused at alarming rates. The lusts of the world entice and deceive. The choices reveal the heart of a person."

Oh God, what is my role in this world?

"My child and chosen one, all one can do is testify to the Truth for the sake of redemption of humanity. When you testify, the power of My Spirit is ushered into the moment. Yes, I can move into people's lives without your testimony. However, your testimony and human engagement brings power and re-enforcement for My plan for humanity. Remember, though you become frustrated and desire to exit this world, I need your help. Your time is not over. There is much left to accomplish on the earth. My ways are not your ways, and My ways include redemption for humanity. Redemption brings Truth where it has been hidden. Redemption is My way. You cannot understand because your humanness supersedes. You desire quick resolve and peace on earth. Peace will come when I return but there is much yet to be done before I return. Seek ye first the kingdom of God and all will be given to you."

Scripture for the day: 2 Corinthians 5:11-21
Beyond the curtain: Get your notebook. Begin writing what comes into your mind and spirit.

Notes:

DAY 65: Pray: Lord Jesus, I come to You today. I need You. I ask for wisdom and discernment. Open my eyes to see and my ears to hear what You have for me today. Thank You, Father. Amen.

"Today is the day the LORD has made. Let us rejoice and be glad in it."

Rejoicing is hard when you are not well.

"Your accuracy is correct but when the rejoicing comes, healing and peace are extended to those who embrace it. All people face difficulty in some way whether it is in the body, soul or life's experiences, or the spirit. The challenges in this realm are part of humanity's experience in the world. When you enter heaven, you are free. You are free from pain and anguish on the earth. Do not forsake the pain. Forsaking pain means you are ignoring its intention. The intention of pain is to draw you closer to Me. Thus, your pain is a tool of dependence upon Me, the one who is the Great Healer and Maker of the earth. The enemy thinks he is the king of the earth, but I AM the Great I Am. I am the Maker of the earth and control all that manifests. It is important to recognize that the earth is not your home. It is only a journey through which you experience. The experience is intended so that you may orchestrate heaven on earth. Remember, it is a temporary experience. Your permanent residence is in heaven."

Do we misunderstand our role and responsibilities on earth?

"Oh, yes, My chosen one. Few engage their true calling in their earthly experience. If one can look beyond their earthly experience, then one can experience true freedom while on the earth. Be reminded that what is around you is merely a temporary cycle to see beyond into the holy of holies."

Scripture for the day: Luke 9:21-27
Beyond the curtain: Journal in your notebook

Notes:

DAY 66: Pray: Lord Jesus, I come to You today. I need You. I ask for wisdom and understanding. Open my eyes to see and my ears to hear what You have for me today. Thank You, Father. Amen.

"It is time. It is time to spread the Good News to all the nations. All people must know of the Kingdom of God. It is My people on the earth who demonstrate who I am. The people of God must arise and stand for the great battle before them. Do not wither and fade away. No! It is time to gather what is needed to do your work, your Kingdom work! Do not forsake one's comfort for what I am asking of you. Your reward will be great! Your reward will come on earth as in heaven."

Lord, it may help us to understand this reward. Can You explain?

"Yes! You will have an earthly reward such as peace and calm. Your greatest reward comes in the heavenly realm where the reward is greater than you could imagine. You will find freedom from all earthly challenges. The authority you accepted on earth is the authority you have in the heavenly realm. There is much to be conveyed regarding the heavenly realm. The heavenly realm holds levels of authority much like you have on earth. The difference between earthly authority and heavenly authority is celebration for your achievement unlike earthly responsibilities which hold burdens and envy. Celebration is a core element of heaven. This cannot be taken from you and is part of the reward. My chosen people, endure through the trials of the earth for great reward will come to those who endure and accomplish My plans through their trials. Stand firm, My children, and do not lose hope for I will return to earth for you."

Scripture for the day: Hebrews 5

Beyond the curtain: Journal in your notebook

Notes:

DAY 67: Pray: Lord Jesus, I come to you today. I need You. I ask You to place Your armor on me (Eph. 6). I praise You.

"My chosen one, there is a battle raging among you. The evil desires your soul. The battle rages but I am greater. I am stronger. I am the Great I Am. Nothing can be greater than Me. Remind yourself that you serve the God who made the earth and the sea. My son came to earth to save your soul. It is through My son that redemption is given, and victory is imminent. Your responsibility is to surrender to Me in all things and I will make Myself known to you. Do not fear, My child. I am with you always. Ask and it will be given. Seek and you will find. There you will always find Me."

God, what is our responsibility in the spiritual battle?

"To always know the battle has been won through Jesus, My son. When you know the battle rages and swarms around you, call on Jesus. When you find yourself tempted, call on Jesus. When you are overwhelmed, call on Jesus. When I call you to fight the battle, call on Jesus to go before you. Be reminded that Jesus came, died, and resurrected from death so that you have His ever presence. This is not a game. This is real and active on the earth. You may laugh when a game is played but the seriousness of this battle is no laughing matter. Why not? Because the battle is over your soul and the souls of others. Put your armor on! Ask Me who you are, and I will not withhold from you. Ask Me what you are to do, and I will not withhold the plans before you. Dear soldier, you are needed in the Kingdom of God. Fight the battle before you. Stand firm in the faith. Join with others to form the Army of God. You will see what can be done, for none is greater. Sweet one, your armor is essential for battle. Do as instructed and place it upon you. Every thought and every emotion are to be surrendered to Me. I will protect you and order your steps."

Scripture for the day: 2 Timothy 2

Beyond the curtain: Journal in your notebook

Notes:

DAY 68: Pray: Lord Jesus, I surrender to You wholly and completely. I ask for wisdom and discernment. Show me Your Truth and Your will. Show me what I cannot see. Help me to walk in the fullness of Your plan for me. Thank You.

"My chosen one, the day before you is lovely and wonderful. Learn to enjoy the beauty of the day – the trees blowing in the wind, the sun as it strikes the water, the calm amidst the chaos. I am there. I am present. You cannot see the goodness of God without sitting with the beauty of these things. I made these things, and they are My gift to you. A gift that is eternal. A gift that is ever present. Do not forsake what I have given."

God, help me to see or hear more of Your beauty that is around me.

"Learn to sit with yourself in My presence without pressure to achieve, accomplish, or do. Be attentive to the workings of My spirit among you. Learn to rest in My presence. Learn to rest under the shadow of the Almighty God. This is My desire for My people."

Scripture: Psalm 91

Beyond the curtain: Psalm 91 begins with "those who live in the shelter of the Most High …" This puts emphasis on our responsibility to sit in His shelter. "Sitting" may look different given the day. Some days may be resting and listening while other days may be doing with a pure heart. Embrace the stage of life you find yourself without condemnation and learn to live in His presence no matter your day.

Notes:

DAY 69: Lord, I struggle to connect and hear Your voice. Please break through.

"I am here. I have not left you nor forsaken you. You are Mine and I am yours. My child, the time is near. The time when many fall to the wayside while others are drawn closer to Me. Those who choose to step away will suffer great consequences. Those who choose Me will find great reward."

Lord, are we in a different season of the world?

"My child, on days when you do not hear Me, you must know I am with you. I am with you in ways that are unseen and unknown. The mind wants to hear but the Spirit wants to reveal. Learn to embrace the Spirit. Learn to live within the Spirit's reach and leadership. This will be uncomfortable for many for they desire understanding and guidance. But the Spirit is like the wind. The wind blows and you do not see it. The wind is still, and you do not see it. In both instances, the wind is present and so is the Spirit. The Spirit was given so that you are not alone. You have an ever-present help. Learn to be attentive to the Spirit as it leads you. The Spirit is trustworthy. For those who have a mustard seed of faith will produce great things. Do not lose hope. Live life and embrace the Spirit among you for it lives within you and among you."

Scripture: I Timothy 3:14-16

Beyond the curtain: Consider what you expect from the Lord such as to hear from Him or see His actions. Expectations bring defeat and pain whether it is human expectations or those placed on God. Learn to live in flow with the Spirit. Living "in flow" or "in movement" with the Spirit allows you to have freedom as well as the Spirit. Transitioning to this lifestyle takes time. Remind yourself it is a journey to enjoy not a rigid existence with demands. Jesus came so we may enjoy freedom on the earth. Give yourself this gift.

Notes:

DAY 70: What is love?

"Love conquers all things. Love is a tool to deconstruct even the most difficult person you face. Love is shown in affection but also through actions and deeds. Love and kindness are different."

Help me understand how love and kindness are different.

"Read 1 Corinthians."

The Apostle Paul addresses the Corinthians rather boldly in 4:18-21. He talks about living by Your power and coming to them with love and a spirit of gentleness despite their arrogant attitudes. This tells me love is power. Love for oneself is addressed in 6:19 where Paul states, "don't you realize that your body is the temple of the Holy Spirit, who lives in you and was given to you by God?" The love we have for ourselves is shown to God by protecting our body as the temple of the Holy Spirit. Chapter 13 presents If-then perspective where the reader is subject to repercussions if love is not extended. In verse 4 of chapter 13, Paul instructs about what love is. Verses 4-7 are powerful and reflect the depth of love that we are called to extend to others. I find it interesting that Paul has the chapter about love located where he does. What do You say, God?

"The importance of love should be demonstrated through the body of Christ, the church. Love overcomes much evil in the world."

How does love conquer evil?

"It is a strategic spiritual move on behalf of My people. I will honor their love for humanity. I will honor their love for themselves. I will honor their love to defend Me. Love is the most powerful tool a Christ follower can carry."

Beyond the curtain:
Who is that difficult person in your life?

How can you extend love to this person? Extending love to a difficult person may look different than extending love to someone you like.

Notes:

DAY 71: What does communion with You look like?

"Communion is an ongoing relationship both in spirit and relationally. Relationally a person interacts with their world through sounds, smells, vision, taste, and touch. I desire to interact with them in the same way. I created their senses. I know the power of them. I may bring an odor, either good or bad, to one's nose and the intent is purposeful for the attention of the person. One must bring awareness into their existence in order to stop and ask My intention. By asking Me, one engages their spirit in connection with My Spirit. When one cultivates this engagement with Me then the communion deepens as would any human relationship."

I am led to read Philemon, a small, one chapter book of the New Testament. This book is rarely considered. However, as I read it a couple times, I see why I was led there. Paul presents a picture of relationship with fellow believers. What a beautiful picture of communion with like-minded friends.

Communion or communication with people is often distorted to present passivity. However, Paul presents a picture of healthy, assertive communication where he greets, presents, requests, comforts, and advocates for Onesimus to Philemon. As we consider communication patterns in our lives, do they present assertiveness? Do they present unhealthy patterns of passivity, aggressiveness, or passive-aggressive behaviors?

Communion with God merges with communication as we extend ourselves from the space of communion into daily interactions with people. Continue to engage communion in your spirit as you interact. You may be shocked with what manifests through your senses.

Beyond the curtain:
Do you exhibit unhealthy communication patterns such as passivity, aggressiveness, or passive-aggressiveness?

Begin a new journey to respond in a healthy response of assertiveness.

Notes:

DAY 72: As I was heading to work this morning, I noticed a young man walking on the side of the road. He had a little mohawk with the sides of his head shaven, some tattoos, and ragged clothing.

Spirit said, *"look at the Person, not the Package."*

How profound is that? The judging spirit is in humanity. We think highly of a handsome man or beautiful woman, but not so much for the average or homely person. Our eyes light up when we see the owner of a stunning new house. Yet, we avert our eyes when coming upon a run-down home. A new car means the owner obviously has it going on, while the person driving a beat-up car needs to adjust their focus to be more successful. These examples add up to one thing, humanity judges on appearances.

We lose sight of the fact that on the inside every single person on the planet is blood, bones, and organs. We are pretty much the same with few variances. We all want love, joy, happiness, security, healthy bodies, and families. As well as a little success along the way. When we judge the outside of the package without ever looking inside, we do ourselves, as well as the person we are judging, a great disservice.

"Instead of reflexively judging someone, taking the time to open the Package just might reveal a truly, amazing Present."

Beyond the curtain: Read Philippians 2. In verse 17, Paul states, "But I will rejoice even if I lose my life …" Do you rejoice when things are going bad? Do you rejoice when there is a job loss, lack of funds to pay the bills, the car breaks down, or troubles persist? Consider rejoicing. It may be a pivotal turning point that pushes you through the pain and into peace, calm, and joy.

Notes:

DAY 73: God, why are You such a mystery to so many? People look for answers to their life's problems. They need healing and comfort. Help me understand.

"People, especially Americanized Christians, expect immediate answers. They want immediate healing, immediate intimacy, immediate financial resolve, immediate everything. They do not understand waiting. They do not understand surrender to the King of kings and Lord of lords. They seek but if they do not find and receive immediately then they believe I am not there. They believe immediacy equates to My presence, My healing, or My favor. They must learn to sit with Me, surrender to Me, trust Me, and fellowship with praise during this time. Oh child, sit and enjoy My presence. Do not place pressure on yourself, another, or Me. By sitting in surrender, you will gain much knowledge and understanding."

Thank You, Father, for sharing Your heart with me. Give me calm in my spirit and soul to sit with You. Teach me to live this way with You. Thank You for Your patience. I love You, Lord.

"Go to your secret place and sit with Me. You will find rest there."

Beyond the curtain: Read Psalm 91. Identify the verse that stands out to you. Memorize this verse. Write it down. Meditate on it. Allow the Spirit to speak into this verse and how it applies to you.

Pray: Dear God, Holy Spirit, Jesus thank You for being with me. I give You praise. You are greater than me for You are God, and I am not. Give my spirit calm so I may sit with my troubles, my pain, and desires. I surrender the desire or needs I yearn to have resolve. Please forgive me. Come Holy Spirit and speak to me.

Notes:

DAY 74: Father, many hearts are wounded, and they see anguish in the world. Negativity precedes them. What am I to do? It seems no matter how I help, their negativity and anguish remain. How do I navigate life with them? What am I to do?

"My child, My child, their pain is deep. Their pain is rooted so deeply that it formed their identity and condemnation permeates their existence. Love covers a multitude of sins (I Peter 4:8). Love is what they need. Love conquers evil. Love shows them another way. Love is greater than anguish, turmoil, and bitterness. Love far exceeds the protective layer they place upon themselves. Consider this layer as it covers the soul of the hurt. A person learns to place the layer so hurt cannot creep upon them any longer. The protection is invisible yet insanely obvious. The layer protects them from others because when they are seen, ridiculed, beaten, and infringed upon in unhealthy ways. These people have few who extend love their way. Love is the answer to permeate the cracks of their protective layer. The ease of this process is not quick nor fanciful, but it is productive over time. Be patient in the process while allowing My Spirit to manifest and heal. Gradually, the layer will thin, and changes will occur. Love is your position."

This is difficult, Lord. It is maddening, frustrating, and exhausting.

"Yes. This you feel compares minimally to the woundedness they have experienced."

Beyond the curtain: Read I Corinthians 13. Write the verses that stand out to you on a note card. Post this note card in a visible location where you are reminded of these verses. Go to the Bible app, make an image to include your verse. Then, put that image on your phone as your screensaver or in a location of visibility.

Notes:

DAY 75: God, what do You desire to speak today?

"I am a mighty God. I do not seek other's opinions. I do not make decisions because others told Me. I am God. I am Yahweh. I am the King of kings and Lord of lords. Humanity assumes I orchestrate My moves for My benefit, but the Truth remains that we are joined in Spirit and in Truth. Humanity is earth's reward so communion may exist between heaven and earth. The earth is Mine. I do not desire to destroy it. I desire to accommodate it. I desire for My creation to commune with Me and My people. You are My people, and you live on the earth for this communion. Learn to commune with Me and with My creation. Your body will benefit from this communion. Great things will come when communion happens. Yes! The Great Awakening upon the earth will move the mountains. The Great Awakening is ready to burst forth with praise! Celebrate with Me. Celebrate with Me, thus saith the Lord!"

How do we commune with Your creation, the earth?

"It is simple. Learn to enjoy what you cannot make for yourself. Learn to enjoy the birds, oceans, animals, rodents, weeds, flowers, bugs, trees, the sky, mountains, lakes, rivers, and the list goes on. These are here for your enjoyment and Mine. These were made for you. They were made for Me. They were made for communion between us all. Communion is relationship between two things. Communion is movement. Movement is initiated. It is time you initiate. Go and do, My child."

Beyond the curtain: Read Genesis 1. Read it slow. Meditate on the significance of its power. Begin with Genesis 1:1-2, "In the beginning God created the heavens and the earth. The earth was formless and empty, and darkness covered the deep waters. And the Spirit of God was hovering over the surface of the waters."

Meditation is slowing the mind/body to connect in your spirit with God's Spirit. Sit in this space with our Father. What do you hear, see, think, feel, or experience?

Notes:

DAY 76: Read Galatians 5 and 6. Consider love, love for others as greater than yourselves. Yet, neglecting oneself is not healthy. However, one is not to boast or make oneself greater than another. As we consider Galatians 5:22, what fruit is evident in your life? Is it love, joy, peace, patience, goodness, faithfulness, gentleness, or self-control? Which do you desire more of? God says in Matthew 7 that if you ask, it will be given. Dear chosen ones, ask God for joy and it will be given. Ask for self-control and it will be given. Be reminded that the Word of God is sharper than a two-edged sword (Hebrews 4:12). Truth will penetrate the dark corners and set you free. "For you have been called to live in freedom, My brothers and sisters" (Galatians 5:13).

"My chosen people, called by My name, I am with you always until the end of the earth. Learn to be free in the Spirit. Learn to live separate from the chains that hold you captive. Learn to live in the freedom that extends to you, the freedom to be who I called you to be. You are Mine and I am yours. Walk in the Truth, chosen one. Walk in humility, not pride. Walk in the goodness of how I created you. Walk as never before and you will experience the peace that passes all understanding (Philippians 4:6-7). I sent My son to give you this freedom. You cannot be free and be in chains. What is it that binds you? Is it lust? Lust of the eyes for what the world lures you? Is it lust for what you do not have? Stand firm, My child. Stand firm in the faith, the Word of God. Stand firm and do not wander, do not walk faintly. I will give you all you need. Ask me."

Beyond the curtain: Consider the lust of the eyes. What do you lust for – money, a car, home, person, a title, child? The list is great. Lust is worldly – and does not fit in God's will. Examine your heart carefully for what you yearn to have. Remind yourself of the contentment that God calls you to. Contentment is shared in Matthew 6:25-26, Philippians 4:12-13, Hebrews 13:5, and I Timothy 6:6-7. There are many more verses. Surrender your will, desire, and passions to God. Ask the Spirit to align these with God's perfect will for you. Allow this surrender to be covered with Christ's sacrifice. Invite God's heavenly army to come around you and protect you.

Notes:

NEXT STEPS:

It is my desire you continue to grow in your relationship with God through the power of His Spirit. Remain attentive to His leading. Journal what He says so it is always available. Care not about what others think of you, for what God thinks of you is all that matters. Our relationship with God may look like madness to the world so fret not, and do not please others but only please our God. Do not forsake spreading the Good News of Jesus Christ, for others need you and your testimony. Be patient with others for we're all on a journey of discovery amidst our hurts and joys. Lastly, love covers a multitude of sins so love one another with grace.

May the power of God fall upon you and direct your steps, may His face shine upon you and give you favor in the days ahead.

                                              Shalom,
                                              Lucinda

ABOUT THE AUTHOR

Lucinda Peters Black grew up in the mountains of Virginia. She remembers listening to Billy Graham on the television and accepting Jesus as her Savior in the 1970s. Her childhood family visited many Christian denominations varying from Presbyterian, Baptist, Methodist, and Pentecostal. As a young adult and mom, she joined the Mennonite church where she remained for many years. Later in life, she experienced additional denominations. Through the many church experiences, she recognizes each denomination varies in custom but the heart of each is to have a relationship with Jesus.

As a young adult and mother, she began cultivating her relationship with God. She sectioned a corner in her dining room, added a rocking chair, and table. This began a lifelong journey with God and learning to distinguish His voice over her own thoughts. She began journaling words from God so she would never forget. She now has a collection of journals with words from God to her. God's words have directed her through motherhood, careers, marriage, divorce, college, relationships, mentoring, and advancing the Kingdom of God.

Lucinda experienced a traumatic divorce in her forties catapulting her desire to follow God no matter where He called her, and she was willing to give up everything to follow Him. At this time, God instructed Lucinda to return to college and get her degree. With only six credits, she entered Johnson Bible College (Johnson University) in Knoxville, Tennessee at the age of 44. She knew no one in the city and started life anew.

Lucinda completed her bachelor's degree in bible and Non-profit Management with a minor in counseling at the age of 48. God asked Lucinda to continue her training by attending graduate school. She graduated at age 50 with her master's degree in Marriage & Family Therapy and Clinical Mental Health Counseling from Johnson University in Knoxville, Tennessee. She continued her training in various forms including EMDR, Splankna, and Green Cross Academy of Traumatology.

Lucinda has a private practice in Knoxville, Tennessee where she assists in trauma recovery with the inclusion of God's healing. God calls Lucinda to travel and pray for revival throughout various regions. It is her prayer that God's will be done on earth as in Heaven.

Lucinda Peters Black, Clinical Traumatologist, MFT/PC
www.therapyfortrauma.com
865-771-2167

Made in the USA
Monee, IL
13 January 2023